FRANCIS MARION

Swamp Fox of the Revolution

The greatest guerrilla fighter in the American Revolution was Francis Marion. Incredibly daring, he terrorized the entire British army in South Carolina, striking with fantastic swiftness, then vanishing ghost-like into the swamps. When Charleston fell to the enemy, Marion escaped and formed Marion's Brigade. The only reward they sought was freedom from tyranny, freedom for America. Although Marion received a Congressional citation, he was never accorded the honor his country owed him, but his brigade earned its rightful place in history.

FRANCIS MARION

Swamp Fox of the Revolution

BY

BERYL WILLIAMS AND SAMUEL EPSTEIN

JULIAN MESSNER   NEW YORK

Published simultaneously in the United States and Canada by
Julian Messner, a division of Simon & Schuster, Inc.,
1 West 39 Street, New York, N.Y. 10018. All rights reserved.

Copyright © 1956 by Beryl Williams and Samuel Epstein

Sixth Printing, 1967

Printed in the United States of America
Library of Congress Catalog Card No. 56–10442

BOOKS BY:

BERYL WILLIAMS
AND
SAMUEL EPSTEIN

FRANCIS MARION: Swamp Fox of the Revolution

THE GREAT HOUDINI: Magician Extraordinary

LILLIAN WALD: Angel of Henry Street

MARCONI: Pioneer of Radio (*pseud. Douglas Coe*)

MEDICINE FROM MICROBES: The Story of Antibiotics

NO PATTERN FOR LOVE

PIONEER OCEANOGRAPHER: Alexander Agassiz

PLANT EXPLORER: David Fairchild

ROAD TO ALASKA (*pseud. Douglas Coe*)

WILLIAM CRAWFORD GORGAS: Tropic Fever Fighter

CHAPTER

I

In the summer of the year 1780 the whole population of London burst into a riot of rejoicing over the news that Charleston, South Carolina, had fallen into British hands and that almost every man of America's Southern Army had become a British prisoner.

Charleston had been the proud heart of Southern resistance to the King's forces. Her downfall meant, to England, the downfall of the whole South and the promise of a swift and victorious end to the entire colonial rebellion. Parliamentary leaders particularly congratulated each other over the message received from Sir Henry Clinton, Charleston's conqueror. "I may venture to assert," Clinton had written, "that there are few men in South Carolina who are not either our prisoners or in arms with us."

Many Americans believed Sir Henry's statement as completely as his fellow Englishmen did. Most people in the Northern colonies had never even heard the names of the scant handful of men who would yet turn the tide of affairs for South Carolina and bring new faith and new strength to the whole rebel cause. They had never heard of Thomas Sumter, of William Richardson Davie, of Andrew Pickens, or of a man named Francis Marion.

Francis Marion, in that year of 1780, was already middle-aged, a small, thin, quiet man with a narrow, thoughtful face.

Planter by choice and by training, he had learned to feel a deep hatred of war's bloodshed and destruction. Men who fought under him from then on stood almost in awe of his bravery; but they said he so seldom drew his sword that it rusted in the scabbard. As a regular soldier, in the years before Charleston's defeat, his strongest weapon had been discipline—the ability to transform the rawest recruits into soldiers who stood firm under fire. Afterward, as a partisan, his weapon was surprise. His habit and his genius then was to lead his ragged Brigade, which received no pay, no food, seldom even any ammunition from the rebel government it was defending, out of its hiding place in the swamps, to strike with terrible and startling swiftness, and to return to the swamps again before the amazed enemy knew what had happened. He never commanded a big army on a large battlefield. He never won a victory in his own name that could be called important.

But during the three long years that dragged by between Charleston's fall and the end of the war, Marion's slight figure grew to the size of a legendary giant in the minds of Patriot and British soldiers alike.

Today little more is known about Francis Marion than most Americans might have learned in 1780. As far as his early life is concerned, there are almost no records, either because they never existed or because they were lost during the war. Marion seems never to have talked very much about himself and to have written very little beyond tersely official military reports and orders.

Some of what is known for certain about him comes from the rather pompous military memoirs of General William Moultrie, who was Marion's superior officer during the years before Charleston's fall—the period when Marion's story is essentially the story of his state and the army it raised to oppose the forces of England. The only firsthand account of Marion's years as a partisan fighter is a little-known book written by William Dobein James, who served under Marion during that time.

But these facts have been amplified by legends, and they

have their importance, too, for they show how people felt about Marion in the days when he was still remembered by those whose homes he had protected, whose lives he had saved. Many of these legends first appeared in print in a biography of Marion written by the itinerant book agent, writer and preacher, Mason L. Weems—the same Parson Weems who invented, for his biography of Washington, that baseless but perhaps nevertheless characteristic story of young George and the cherry tree. There is no way of knowing just which incidents Weems invented for the Marion biography. He claimed he wrote the book from material furnished by Peter Horry, one of Marion's closest friends and most faithful followers. He even used Horry's name on the title page along with his own. But Horry said when he saw the book, "Most certainly 'tis not my history, but your romance."

Weems wrote that "this great soldier, at his birth, was not larger than a New England lobster, and might easily enough have been put into a quart pot." It is not a statement that anyone today can prove or disprove. But it is a reminder of what was undoubtedly true: that Marion's slightness as a man aroused no condescension among the bigger, brawnier men with whom he fought. His enemies regarded him with an almost superstitious fear, his friends with a kind of marveling pride.

Weems also says that as a boy of twelve Marion embarked on a voyage to the West Indies in a schooner that was "suddenly attacked by some monstrous fish." As the vessel sank, Weems says, Marion and the crew escaped into a small boat, to drift for eleven days under a broiling tropical sun with no water and no food except the "raw flesh" of the ship's little dog. On the tenth day "the captain and mate leaped overboard, raving mad; and the day following the two remaining seamen expired in the bottom of the boat." Shortly thereafter a passing ship rescued young Marion, sole survivor of the shipwrecked group, and its captain nursed him back to health with "chocolate and turtle broth." When he had returned to his home, Weems concluded, "Marion never thought of another trip to sea."

William Dobein James, author of the *Sketch of the Life of Brig. Gen. Francis Marion and a History of His Brigade*, tells the sea voyage story too, from facts he said he obtained from "an early friend" of Marion's. His version is less dramatic. In it the young sailor was sixteen years old, and he reached safety after only seven days in an open boat.

But once again Weems' story, legend or not, points up a characteristic that was outstanding in Francis Marion: the incredible endurance he showed throughout his wartime career. While men younger and apparently much stronger than himself were falling by the roadside, begging for a ration of rice and the opportunity to rest, Marion was still upright in his saddle, urging them on, as if rest and food were trivial luxuries he could do without for days on end.

James' book too is probably sometimes misleading. He joined Marion's famous Brigade when he was a boy of fifteen. He wrote his *Sketch* after Marion's death and when he himself must have been nearing sixty. Yet even then he still felt a small boy's hero worship for his commander—an attitude that is likely to overlook faults and magnify virtues. But, like a Weems invention, this attitude points up the fact that though Marion's Brigade often fought without support and with almost no recognition, its members felt toward Marion himself a loyalty and admiration that few leaders ever inspire.

A British commander's hatred has added one more stroke to the picture of Marion that has come down to us. "The Swamp Fox," Lieutenant Colonel Banastre Tarleton called him, furious at the American for again eluding the redcoats. The phrase was intended as an insult, but Marion's followers adopted it with pride and it remains the name by which Marion is still best known. It was a fitting description, his Brigade thought, of a leader who could use swiftness and strategy in place of the fighting power he lacked, who was constantly pursued by his enemies but never fell into their hands.

From the books of Weems and James, then, from letters, from memoirs of other outstanding figures of the Revolution (especially Tarleton himself, Moultrie, and "Light Horse" Harry Lee), from hints to be found in Marion's French Huguenot background and in the whole period of colonial and Revolutionary history through which he lived, we must try to form our own opinion of the man as he must have been.

We seldom know what he thought, because he customarily kept his thoughts to himself. But we do know some of the things he did and what certain other people thought about him. And they are enough to suggest, at least, why the story of Francis Marion, though it may never be complete, is still a favorite chapter in America's own story of her fight for freedom.

CHAPTER

II

In the same way that the phrase "Swamp Fox" tells something about Marion, the French word *Huguenot* tells something about his family, and especially about his grandfather, Gabriel Marion, the first Marion to settle in the New World.

Huguenots were French Protestants. For more than a century and a half, by Gabriel Marion's time, they had clung stubbornly to their belief that a man had a right to interpret the New Testament according to his own understanding and not by the doctrine imposed by the Pope and his hierarchy. France was a Catholic country and they suffered for their belief. But confiscation of their property, imprisonment and even sentence of death failed to shake them.

Then, in 1685, King Louis XIV ruled that every Protestant in France must either accept the Catholic creed or be banished. For most Huguenots the choice was immediate. They had long ago accepted the fact that men who insisted upon their right to think as they liked had to pay for that right in one way or another. Within the next few years four hundred thousand of them, including some of the King's bravest and ablest subjects, sailed away into exile. Among the hundred or so families who sought haven in the new British colony of Carolina were young Gabriel Marion and his wife Louisa.

Most of the trained artisans among them settled in Carolina's one real town, Charleston—or Charles Town, as it was then called—on the low spit of land between the mouths of the Ashley and the Cooper rivers. Charleston was less than twenty years old at the time, but it already wore an air of surprising stability. This was partly because it had quickly established trade with Indian tribes as far west as the Mississippi, which supplied thousands of fine furs for sale to England. But it was also because many of Charleston's residents had come to Carolina after having lived in the much older British colony of Barbados.

On that rich Caribbean island those English-born settlers had learned the habits of a leisurely life based on slave labor, and they had brought both the habits and the slaves with them to their new homes. They built elaborate gardens beneath Charleston's characteristic palmetto trees and furnished their handsome homes with imported furniture. They were the first American colonists to organize a public library and establish a theater. Even in 1690 Charleston was showing signs of the culture that would make it remarkable among the pioneer settlements along the Atlantic coast. The new French-speaking families who arrived there found themselves accepted in this miniature metropolis with sophisticated aplomb.

But the farmers among the Huguenots had to make their homes in a less welcoming environment, along one or another of Carolina's many seaward-flowing rivers. Those rivers were the colony's main arteries of transportation. The flat, marshy, island-tipped peninsulas, into which they fringed the coastline, would someday soon bear rich crops of rice and indigo—indigo for valuable dyes, rice to fill the holds of ships sailing around Africa to India and the Far East, and returning by way of Africa again to pick up cargoes of slaves.

When the Huguenots arrived, however, rice had not yet built wealthy river-front plantations, and indigo was not yet being cultivated. And though they settled no more than twenty miles inland—for several years yet Carolina would have no settlements farther west than that—even that slight distance brought them into an empty wilderness that had to be tamed and brought to fertility by their own hands and their own labor. They had no slaves to help them. Most of the Huguenots, because they had lost their money when they had lost their right to live in France, could not even afford the tools and implements that would have eased their labor. In self-contained little communities they established themselves along the Santee some miles north of Charleston and on the banks of the Cooper River and its tributary, Goose Creek. Gabriel Marion was of this group.

How Gabriel Marion went about clearing his grant of land or raising his first home in the wilderness is not known. He had been a farmer in La Rochelle, in western France, and his tract along Goose Creek gave him easy passage to Charleston by water. Perhaps his experience and his location made him luckier than most, though this hardly suggests a life of ease. Peter Horry, Francis Marion's friend and fellow officer, could remember hearing how his own Huguenot grandfather and grandmother labored together at the whipsaw, cutting rough planks out of felled trees. But by the time of his death, at least, Gabriel Marion had achieved some prosperity.

"As to the wealth with which God has been pleased to bless me and my dear Louisa and children," his will read, "lovingly have we labored together for it—lovingly have we enjoyed it—and now, with a glad and grateful heart do I leave it among them."

Gabriel's oldest son, also named Gabriel, became Francis Marion's father. When he married Esther Cordes, daughter of another Huguenot family, he settled in what was known as St. John's parish of Berkeley County, the county which on its coastal edge included Charleston itself. There his children were born—five sons and one, or as some historians say, two daughters. The four eldest sons, Gabriel, Isaac, Benjamin and Job, all, Weems wrote, "bought farms—proved their oxen—married wives—multiplied good children." Francis, the last born, became a planter too—a good planter, folks always said.

Admirers of Francis Marion usually declare that he was born in 1732, the same year in which George Washington was born, and take pleasure in pointing out this coincidence of birthdays for the two Revolutionary heroes. But the truth is he may have been born the following year. All we have to go on is the carving on Marion's tombstone, which says that he died in February of 1795 "in the sixty-third year of his age."

When he was six or seven years old his father moved to another farm or plantation on Winyah Bay, near the settlement of Georgetown that had been laid out only two or three years before.

Georgetown's broad streets formed large uniform squares, and it already had a brick bank building along its Front Street. There were stores on that street too, with wharves at their backs for the delivery of goods from nearby plantations. Four rivers, the Waccamaw, the Big Pee Dee, the Sampit, and the Black, all emptied into Winyah Bay, flooding its banks into marshland that was fragrant with yellow jasmine, sweet bay and heavy-scented magnolia. Water lilies and blue water hyacinths grew in still, dark pools, and the branches of towering cypresses were heavy with drifting gray scarves of moss.

Probably, like most boys of that day, Marion learned at home to read and write and do sums. Also, like most boys, he probably joined his father and brothers in the fields as soon as he was able, and learned the rudiments of farming before he made that single and disastrous trip to sea.

By the time Francis Marion was twenty-five he and his brother Gabriel were working together. Their father had died by then. Their mother lived with them. Probably all her other children were already married and in homes of their own.

The next year, in 1759, Francis apparently went off on his own to work the plantation he bought some years later for the sum of eight hundred pounds. It was a pleasant tract of two hundred acres near the south bank of the Santee, with a pond at the foot of a bluff overlooking the river. Marion called it Pond Bluff. There he was once more a resident of the parish of St. John's, where his father had once lived. Perhaps he thought he would spend the rest of his life in comfortable anonymity, hunting and fishing in his spare time, industriously tending his fields as his father and grandfather had done before him. His life seemed very like his grandfather's, in fact, except that he owned a few slaves—Negro workmen whom, Peter Horry made a point of recording, Marion treated with great humanity. One of those slaves would accompany Marion as cook and companion during all the rigors of his years as a partisan.

Those years were still far in the future. No Carolina colonists, and certainly no respectable and peaceable Huguenots, had yet so much as muttered of independence from England. But they were, in 1759, muttering against the recent massacres by the Cherokees, and it was against these Indians that Marion would first bear arms and win his first laurels as a soldier.

CHAPTER

III

Indian fighting had not been a common experience for the young South Carolinians of Francis Marion's generation. It was their fathers and grandfathers who had fought against the various tribes originally inhabiting their colony, defeating the weaker, causing some to emigrate to other territories, and finally winning the alliance and the profitable trade of most that remained their neighbors.

Of those neighbors, the Cherokees, who could muster six thousand warriors in an emergency, were the most powerful and the most advanced. Their leaders knew that in many ways the white settlers were a threat to the Indians' way of life. But the Cherokees, too, found the fur trade profitable, because they had fine hunting grounds in their vast territory that covered what is now western South Carolina, and parts of North Carolina, Virginia and Georgia. As proof of their friendliness toward the English they had sold the province of South Carolina a tract of land near their own village of Keowee, on the vulnerable eastern border of their lands. On that site, in 1753, the Carolinians had built Fort Prince George, intended as a refuge for white and Indians alike in case of attack by Spaniards from the south or French from the west.

But the barracks and log palisades of Fort Prince George were not very well constructed, and within a few years that symbol of white and Indian amity began to crumble away. Not long afterward the friendly relations between South Carolinians and Cherokees were also crumbling into the mistrust and ill feeling that finally resulted in bloody war.

That deterioration began during the Seven Years' War—sometimes called the French and Indian War—which broke out between England and France in 1756. By the spring of 1761 England was sending a strong British force to aid South Carolina in putting an end to French-inspired Indian attacks. Serving with those British regulars was a regiment of South Carolina volunteers that would be remembered, in the words of one historian, as "the school in which several of the most distinguished officers of the Revolution learned their first lessons in the art of war."

Francis Marion was one of those officers. So was William Moultrie who would command the defense of Charleston against the British during the Revolution. So were Andrew Pickens and Isaac Huger (English-born Carolinians pronounced his name U-gee), both Huguenots like Marion and both, like him, destined for dramatic roles against the British beside whom they now fought.

This was not actually Marion's first foray against the Cherokees. In 1759 he and one of his brothers had taken part in an expedition into the Indian country under William Lyttleton, then Carolina's governor. But that expedition had done no fighting, had been more terrorized by a small pox epidemic in their own ranks than by the presumed enemy—had accomplished little, in fact, beyond proving Lyttleton's inability to deal with the Indians.

The expedition of 1761 was a very different affair. By then the ineffectual Lyttleton's place was filled by William Bull, Carolina's energetic native-born lieutenant governor. Bull had already obtained British regulars for one campaign against the Cherokees when they threatened the frontier settlements in revenge for grievances blamed—and not without reason—on their white neighbors. That campaign in 1760 had resulted in the burning of several villages in the Cherokees' beautiful Keowee valley. When the Indians, newly armed and encouraged by the French, retaliated by destroying one Carolina fort and threatening a second, Fort Prince George, Bull had acted firmly again. At his request the British force arrived, headed by Lieutenant Colonel James Grant, and by his authority Grant's force was assembled.

Grant's army numbered about twenty-six hundred men, including his own Highlanders, the volunteer Provincial Regiment and a few Chicasaw and Catawba allies. In good order they marched westward out of Charleston one spring day in 1761, and on May 7 they reached Fort Prince George. There they rested and took on provisions for thirty days. On June 7 they started through the area of the "lower settlements," those easternmost Cherokee villages deserted since the burnings of the year before.

Each day the trail grew more rugged, the streams more difficult to ford. Ever since they had crossed the Congaree they had been moving through ranges of hills. Now these hills were becoming steeper. This was new country for most of the men— real Cherokee country, which few whites had ever visited except for those hardy wanderers whose business was the Indian fur trade. The soldiers began to listen for war whoops beneath every bird call and imagined dusky-skinned warriors lurking behind every boulder. The stories they told each other about Cherokee scalpings grew more fantastic and more frightening each evening, and the shadows outside the circle of the campfires seemed more menacing each night.

Early one morning, in a narrow line of march that strung out behind a vanguard of Chicasaws and Catawbas, the men moved forward into a valley. It was so dense with thicket that they could scarcely force their way through in single file. To their right and just ahead of them rose a hill. The invisible trail they were following, like the muddy river beside them, curled around the foot of that hill. Burdened with packs and guns, in uniforms too heavy for the valley's steamy heat, the soldiers struggled ahead at little more than a snail's pace.

Then it happened, the moment which they had been half fearing, half anticipating, during all the long, weary days and nights since they had left the coast.

"Cherokees!" The Chicasaws and Catawbas in the van flashed the warning back along the line. "Cherokees on the hill!"

It was too late for concealment. Almost instantly the full fire of the enemies' French guns rained down upon the foremost ranks, frozen where they stood.

Retreat was impossible. Grant would not have permitted it in any case. Beyond that hill lay the Cherokees' mountain-protected "middle settlements," where the greatest part of the nation's population was concentrated. Those settlements were the goal of his expedition.

"Stand and fire!" he commanded. "Stand and fire!"

With sweaty hands provincial volunteers fumbled for bullets, for powder and for wadding. Before their first shots rang out, the Cherokees were upon them, rushing down the hill like an engulfing wave. Some white men fell without so much as having raised their muskets. Others pushed forward to take their places. The rattle of fire grew louder and steadier.

Then, almost as swiftly as they had appeared, the fluid ranks of the Cherokees dissolved back into the forested hillside.

Grant stifled the half-incredulous shouts of victory. He knew the Indians' retreat was merely a ruse intended to draw more British and American soldiers onto the portion of the trail that lay directly at the foot of the hill. He knew, too, that the Cherokees on that hill were almost certainly a picked band of braves stationed at that strategic spot to massacre any white force that tried to reach the middle settlements.

Grant's dilemma proved Marion's first opportunity to distinguish himself. When the British commander decided upon a plan of action, he summoned the young lieutenant from St. John's parish rather than one of his own Highlanders. Marion's orders were to lead a force of thirty men up the hill and assault the Indians in the natural fortress where they had taken refuge.

From that moment on events moved with a desperate rapidity.

Unhesitatingly young Lieutenant Marion led his men straight into the narrow defile that gave the only access to the hill's upper slopes. War whoops sounded in his ears even as he felt the walls of the chasm close about him. The Cherokees fired down from above. They leaped boldly from the rim of the crevasse and bore the white men to earth with their own weight and the fierce blows of their tomahawks. Within a few minutes twenty-one of Marion's thirty men had fallen.

Marion and the remaining nine stood firm. Supporting forces joined them from the rear. At bayonet point they pushed the Cherokees back—only to find the Indians attacking again on their flanks with undiminished valor.

For four hours the fighting raged furiously. No matter how many times the Cherokees appeared to retreat, they always rallied in force from some unexpected direction.

But Grant was as fiercely determined to force the pass as the Cherokees were to prevent him. He sent wave after wave of reinforcements onto the hill, where Marion and the few men with him fought steadily. Under the young lieutenant's direction the troops made skillful use of every boulder and bush as cover. In less than the space of a single morning Marion had absorbed the techniques of Indian fighting. And so determined and steadfast was his own behavior that his men took courage from his presence.

By noon the firing finally slackened. Two hours later it ceased altogether. The Cherokees abandoned the hill and left the pass below it open to the invaders.

Grant wasted no time on celebration and little more on his wounded. As soon as his scattered men could be collected again he led them forward. That same night they reached the important Cherokee village of Etchoee some miles beyond the pass. At midnight Grant attacked.

His sudden onslaught met no resistance. Etchoee's huts and its dome-roofed town house were empty, its streets deserted. The Cherokees had left it undefended as if in silent admission of their white enemies' superiority. Grant ordered his men to burn the town to the ground.

Thereafter, for thirty days, Grant marched from one Indian town to another, repeating the pattern of that night's fiery work. No single village made a stand in its own defense. Instead the Indian population fled into the mountains at the white men's approach. But silent flight did not satisfy Colonel Grant. At each of the Indians' fourteen settlements he issued orders for burning the town house and the family huts, the granary, the livestock pens, and the fields that surrounded the village—the rows of straight green corn and the bean vines customarily planted among them. The charred and smoking ruins he left behind, on that grim journey of destruction, would furnish no shelter and no food for the Cherokees for many months to come.

Marion was a seasoned soldier by the end of that month. He had learned techniques of fighting that he would use with brilliant effect during his years as a partisan. But he had not learned to enjoy destruction.

When the campaign was over and Colonel Grant marched his men victoriously back to the coast, Marion returned gratefully to the task of cultivating his own beloved and familiar acres overlooking the Santee. He was to see a good deal more of war in his lifetime, but he would never be able to find pleasure in destroying what other men—enemies or not—had sown and tended with the hopeful labor that every planter knew. He was glad to be a planter again. In his own eyes he would always be a planter.

CHAPTER

IV

In the fourteen years following the French and Indian War—and Carolina's war with the Cherokees that had been part of that struggle—Francis Marion rode downriver to Charleston on many occasions. Sometimes he went to superintend the sale of produce from Pond Bluff Plantation, around which his whole life centered, sometimes to buy farm equipment or supplies for his bachelor household. But when he rode downriver early in January of the year 1775 he had a new and different purpose. He was going to Charleston to take his seat in South Carolina's first Provincial Congress.

Similar congresses were meeting, at about the same time, in almost every American colony, and representatives from most colonies, including South Carolina, were attending the first Continental Congress in Philadelphia. At some of those sessions a few daring men actually mentioned the word "independence," and declared that Americans would be better off if they rid themselves of British rule. Wherever such talk was heard, it was regarded as wildly radical. There was no such talk at all in Carolina.

It is true that Carolinians had objected to certain British officials sent across the Atlantic to govern them or preside over their courts. Many of them had also resented the Stamp Act of 1765, because they thought the British Parliament had no right to levy taxes against colonists. But in 1775 most Carolinians

[23]

were still staunchly loyal to the King. They thought of their colony as having been especially favored by the crown, and believed they owed England thanks for her prosperity.

Certainly she had been prosperous since the end of the Indian fighting. Her many rivers had become busy trade routes for the abundant crops of rice and indigo her marshy peninsulas produced. The ports of Charleston, Beaufort and Georgetown displayed new wealth every year in the form of magnificent homes and handsome public structures.

The colony's population had grown too, along with her wealth. In the Up Country district, as the Low Country or coast-dwelling people called the hilly inland area, there were so many new settlements of Germans, Scottish, Irish and French, each group living rather strictly to itself, that Charlestonians didn't even try to keep track of their numbers. Rich planters were importing slaves so rapidly that the Negro population—it totaled one hundred ten thousand by 1773—had come to outnumber the white two to one.

Under the circumstances South Carolina's Provincial Congress was not called for the redress of her own grievances, because she had too few. It was called chiefly to show sympathy for that less well-favored colony, Massachusetts, whose port of Boston had been declared closed as punishment for resistance to England's tax laws. Once the Congress opened, however, and its members voted that South Carolina should cancel all trade with England as long as Parliament continued to impose taxes on Americans, the colony found itself swept up into the train of events that led inevitably to revolution. But at first even the most ardent delegates had no idea where that train would lead them.

Francis Marion, his brother Job, and their neighbor William Moultrie, seated together as delegates from St. John's parish, were certainly not in favor of war with England when they approved that trade embargo. They were trying to find a peaceable means for discouraging England's highhandedness, which troubled all the colonies, though South Carolina less than most. When they helped set up committees to prevent the sailing and arrival of ships, and to correspond with other colonies on mutual problems, when they voted that every man in the colony should be "diligently attentive in learning the use of arms," they were merely taking precautions.

A few months later—while Marion was back home again and drilling his fellow farmers every two weeks—certain members of the Congress broke into the royal armory in Charleston's state house at night and removed guns, cutlasses and a supply of flints and matches. Even this extreme measure was not meant as a prelude to war. The arms were stolen, not because the colonists might use them against the British, but rather to prevent the British from firing on Americans.

Up in Massachusetts, however, the collection of a supply of arms by Patriots—as men of anti-British sentiments were beginning to be called—had a violent result. News of the pitched battle on Lexington green, between redcoats and colonial farmers, reached Marion's brother Isaac at his home in Little River, on the northern border of South Carolina, early in May. Isaac was a member of a correspondence committee, and the dispatch that came to him had been sent south by galloping horsemen riding in relays. A covering note handed to Isaac at the same time read, "I know you stand in need of no prompting when your country requires your service." Isaac sent the dispatch on with a scrawled message urging hasty delivery to Charleston "for the good of your country, and the welfare of our lives, liberties and fortunes." Seventeen days after the fighting on Lexington green, Charleston learned that the Revolution in the colonies had actually begun.

Summoned to a special meeting of the South Carolina Provincial Congress, Marion and his brother Job rode downriver to Charleston again on June 1. Most Carolinians still didn't want to fight England. People in the Up Country, in fact, scarcely knew or cared what the quarrel was about. But Francis and Job Marion agreed with their brother Isaac that the time had come to risk their lives, if necessary, in defense of the liberties that the New World had always represented to their

Huguenot family. If the soldiers of the King of England were prepared to fight Americans, then Americans must be ready to stand and face them.

The feeling the Marion brothers shared was also the feeling of the Provincial Congress as a whole. Reluctant as its members were to admit that war existed between England and themselves, they now had no other choice. The only problem on which they differed, at first, was how to raise the army they knew they might need at any moment. Some suggested calling out the militia. Others pointed out that the militia, organized under royal government, included Tories, or pro-British sympathizers, as well as Patriots, and that therefore it could not be depended on in the crisis that lay ahead. So the Congress decided to elect by ballot enough officers for three regiments, two of infantry and one of horse, and to turn over to them the job of recruiting individual companies. Men willing to serve as officers were invited to step forward, and the balloting began. The third captain to be elected, out of twenty chosen altogether, was Francis Marion. He was assigned to the Second Regiment, of which William Moultrie was named colonel.

In June of 1775, for the first time in many years, Francis Marion was in uniform again—a new blue uniform this time.

With him, when he set out for Georgetown to fill the ranks of his company, was another newly elected captain, Peter Horry. Younger, livelier, less thoughtful than Marion, Horry looked forward to "marching, fighting, killing, and taking prisoners" as a great adventure. They had to borrow money for the payment of their new recruits, because the sum Congress had voted for their use had not yet been collected. What they wanted was "hard money"—gold or silver, as opposed to the fluctuating paper currency of the day—"and hard money it was indeed," Horry complained. "For two whole days, and with every effort we could make, we collected but the pitiful sum of one hundred dollars!"

The recruiting itself was easier. Marion already had the ability to make men trust him and willingly follow his leadership. By midsummer the two captains had each filled his roster of sixty men and together they marched their new companies back to Charleston.

The city was alive with rumors. Word had come south that just outside of Boston a group of ragged recruits bearing the fine new title of Continental Army had fought the bloody battle of Bunker Hill. Carolina half feared, half looked forward to a similarly bloody battle on her own soil. Men expected the British warship in Charleston harbor to attack the city at night. They told each other that there were still many Tories, especially in the Up Country, and that they would join in such an attack with guns supplied by the royal governor. They suspected the British of arming Indians and urging them to renew their old hostilities against the colonists.

Marion and his fellow members of the Congress signed an agreement declaring their unity with those Bunker Hill Patriots, and their belief that they were "justified before God and man, in resisting force by force." But the rumors of attack came to nothing. No force was exerted against Carolina's newly formed regiments. The colony was no longer at peace, but neither was she actively at war.

In September, Charleston's nervous Council of Safety ordered Moultrie to seize Fort Johnson, the little island fort that guarded the city's harbor. Marion's company was one of three chosen to cross the harbor by night and open a predawn attack. Stealthily they set out in a commandeered packet boat. They found the fort entirely deserted—and learned later that day that the royal governor himself had fled to the safety of the warship *Tamar*. Again Carolinians had been braced for a battle that failed to materialize.

That autumn Marion learned the difficulties of maintaining morale among soldiers whom no enemy ever openly threatened. The only land force England had in the colonies then was cooped up in Boston, apparently afraid to march against the Patriots now commanded by General George Washington, encamped outside the city. Even the patient commander-in-chief was growing discouraged trying to "persuade" his Continentals, as one historian put it, to become an army. Carolina officers were even more discouraged.

A small part of their little force was stationed at Dorchester, a village then situated about twenty miles inland from Charleston, where the Patriots' arms and ammunition were stored. The larger part, numbering a scant five hundred men, built a new camp for themselves on James Island around little Fort Johnson, which was now flying the first American banner seen in South Carolina. The flag had a blue ground, like the blue uniforms of the regiments, and a silver crescent like the one the men wore in their hats. After a time Moultrie could say that his Second Regiment was "well armed, well accoutered, and well clothed, with a sufficient number of regular good tents."

Captain Marion knew, however, that uniforms and arms do not make soldiers. He shook his head over young recruits who seemed to learn nothing but clever excuses for winning themselves an evening's leave in Charleston. Quietly, in his own way, he set about teaching them the discipline that would soon make the Second Regiment famous. His success with a certain dandified lieutenant, devoted to nothing but the sport of cockfighting, was typical of his unorthodox methods.

The lieutenant had already fooled a dozen superiors and was convinced that Marion would be more gullible than them all. Confidently he asked for a leave to visit a sick father invented for the occasion. Just as he had expected, he received Marion's sympathetic permission to go. The trick had worked so well that the young man was in no hurry to return, especially as there were a good many fine cockfights to be seen in that season. Two weeks went by before he presented himself again in Marion's tent, his face pulled long and his excuse ready on his lips. His father's condition, he said, had made it impossible to leave the poor man's bedside any sooner.

The men seated there in the tent with Marion watched their captain carefully as the young man talked. They didn't know whether Marion, so completely honest himself, could see through the polished performance.

Captain Marion didn't answer his visitor immediately. He appeared to be too busy with the papers in front of him even to notice the newcomer's presence. Finally he lifted his head.

"Oh, lieutenant," he said, "is that you? Has it really been two weeks since you left? Well, never mind." He looked down at his papers again. "There's no harm done. I never missed you."

The young lieutenant stared, gulped once, gulped again and fled without a word.

The men around Marion could scarcely contain their explosive laughter. No other officer in the regiment had ever made the slightest dent in that young officer's complacency. Yet with a mere dozen words, with no threat of punishment, their quiet captain had reduced him to gaping wordlessness.

For days the lieutenant was taunted with reminders that "The captain never missed you! He didn't even notice you were gone!" The joke wore thin because after a time the lieutenant no longer responded to it. He suddenly became busy with requisitions, lists and details he had always ignored in the past. For the first time in his military career, he was attending to duty. Marion had transformed him into a soldier.

Winter dragged by there on James Island. Every rumor of attack continued to dwindle away into nothingness. In the spring word spread that England was sending a vast fleet to America to destroy the whole country, and that the fleet would attack the Southern colonies first. But by then so many rumors had already proved baseless that many people thought this one too should be ignored.

Wealthy Charlestonians, however, had a premonition that this one—more frightening than all the rest—might actually be reliable. Their pride told them that if England planned a large-scale attack on America, she would aim her first serious blow at the rich South. A British defeat of Charleston, they believed, would earn more prestige and wealth for England than she could hope to obtain by a victory over any other American city. The anxiety spread. With it spread the grim realization that except for Fort Johnson, Charleston had no real defenses at all.

"We'll reinforce Fort Johnson," Colonel Moultrie said calmly. "We'll fortify Sullivan's Island on the other side of the harbor. We'll mount guns at every wharf around the edge of the city."

Almost overnight all of Charleston and all the soldiers at her command organized themselves into a huge work party. At its head was John Rutledge, once a steadfast moderate in all dealings with England but now engaged with all his will in the protection of his homeland. Rutledge had been accepted for some time as a leader among Carolinians. Now he was their official leader. The Council of Safety, the Provincial Congress and the other makeshift arrangements by which Patriots had previously conducted their business had just been replaced by a new constitutional government. New courts had been set up, paper currency issued, a new legislative assembly elected—Marion was once again a representative from St. John's—and Rutledge had been named His Excellency the President of South Carolina. It was in this new role that he told his people, "The eyes of Europe, nay of the whole world, are on America. The eyes of every other colony are on this."

While civilians ripped the lead sash weights out of their windows to be melted down for musket balls, and contributed their letter paper for the making of cartridges, Marion—he was Major Marion now—established himself on Sullivan's Island, southernmost of the row of long, narrow islands that rims the Carolina coast northward from Charleston. Sullivan's Island was to the seaward of James Island. It would be the first target of an attacking fleet. South Carolina planned to make it her first line of defense.

CHAPTER

V

On June 1 a British fleet, fifty sail in all, appeared directly off Charleston. Riding at anchor beyond the bar, waiting for favorable weather in order to come closer in, the big-gunned warships looked enormous. Among them were transports enough to carry several thousand soldiers.

Three days later Major General Charles Lee arrived from the North, sent to Charleston by Washington himself to aid in the city's defense. Lee's hawk-nosed arrogance bore out his reputation as a soldier who had distinguished himself in many armies in Europe. So did his sharp, scornful voice when he declared himself shocked and horrified by what he saw on his first visit to Sullivan's Island.

Original plans for the fort being constructed there called for a double-walled square, large enough to accommodate a thousand men. The walls were to be built of the spongy palmetto trees that grew in abundance on the island's sandy dunes. The sixteen-foot space between the walls was to be filled with sand. Platforms inside the walls and on the towers at each corner were to serve as gun emplacements. Work had begun first on the two side walls that met at the corner facing the island's southern tip, directly overlooking the city, but the work had gone slowly. Illness, unseasonal heat and lack of sufficient tools had delayed the struggling soldiers and the Negro slaves planters had contributed for their aid. When Lee arrived to inspect the place, not even the first two walls were finished. He spoke his mind on the subject in no uncertain terms.

"The General says our fort is a 'slaughter pen,' " Moultrie reported to Marion and his other officers after Lee had returned to Charleston, where men were bustling their wives and children into carriages for hasty departures inland, and merchants were barricading their shops. "He says," Moultrie continued, "that we ought to withdraw the garrison and give it up immediately. What do you say, eh?" Moultrie's round red face looked angry.

"What does President Rutledge say?" someone asked.

"He doesn't agree."

"Then we don't either."

And so, against Lee's advice, in all but outright opposition to a world-famous general's orders, they decided to stay where they were. There were only some three hundred men in the little incomplete fortress. Another seven hundred and fifty soldiers, including part of the Continental Army sent down from North Carolina and Virginia to aid their sister colony in this crisis, were encamped on the northern end of Sullivan's Island. In Moultrie's opinion this combined force would be sufficient for the fort's defense, even if the British transports landed the three thousand troops he believed they had aboard. Moultrie declared, in fact, that he felt himself perfectly easy.

On June 7 a small boat was rowed out from one of the British men-of-war, heading for Sullivan's Island and bearing a white flag. A nervous sentry, so new to warfare that he didn't recognize the signal for peaceful communication, fired on sight. The boat scurried back to the shelter of its ship's guns.

Moultrie sent an officer out to apologize for the shot and to express his willingness to receive any message the British might care to send. The message came and Moultrie handed it on to Rutledge. It was a proclamation offering free pardon, in His Majesty's name, to all Americans willing to lay down their arms and submit to his government. Charleston—all Carolina, as far as the busy city knew at that moment—ignored it to a man.

The very next day British troops, three thousand strong,

landed on Long Island, the next low, sandy stretch just north of Sullivan's Island and separated from it only by a narrow inlet usually not more than a few feet deep. While they set up camp there, and built works for their mortars and cannon, the Americans facing them across that inlet prepared for instant trouble.

In the meantime Lee was bombarding Moultrie and his staff with a series of frenzied dispatches expressing his conviction that the still-unfinished fort would have to be abandoned at the moment of attack. First he asked that a bridge be built across the mile of water from Sullivan's Island to the mainland, to supply Moultrie's men with a way of retreat. Forced to agree that there was no longer time to undertake such an enormous project—the British men-of-war had crossed the bar and now stood just three miles from Moultrie's post—Lee then insisted that a pontoon causeway, at least, be erected. Valuable manpower was spent gathering empty hogsheads and joining them together with planks. But the first men who tried to cross from one floating hogshead to the next found the makeshift causeway sinking so quickly under their feet that they barely got back to shore. Sullivan's Island remained cut off from the city. Only Moultrie himself and those with him seemed to feel that they were not doomed to destruction.

The sun that June blazed furiously in the sky. The little fort rose slowly, by inches. An experienced sea captain, visiting Moultrie and his staff one day, said gloomily, "When those ships come to lay alongside of your fort, they will knock it down in half an hour."

"In that case," Moultrie told him, "we will lay behind the ruins and prevent their men from landing."

Now, at every point around the city, at the head of every wharf, soldiers were doing extra guard duty and straining their ears for the first sound of gunfire.

It came on the morning of June 28, only a few hours after an exasperated Lee had decided to remove Moultrie from his command. The letter informing Moultrie of his dismissal was never sent. Moultrie would have been too busy to read it if it had reached him. He was riding out to inspect the men encamped at the far end of the island, and grumbling over a bad attack of the gout, when he saw the men-of-war loose their topsails. Instantly he whipped his horse back through the dunes to order his own men to their battle posts.

The drummer boy rolled a loud summons. Gunners hurried to carry ammunition from the magazine for their thirty-one guns. Young recruits clenched their jaws to keep their teeth from chattering, and even the few veterans among them looked pale and spoke in husky voices. Their fort still had only two towers and two real walls. If the British sailed past it and rounded the point of the island to attack it from the rear, as Lee insisted they would do, the garrison would have almost no protection at all.

But they looked at Moultrie, his round face ruddy with the heat and the pain of his gout, and at Marion's dark, thin face, quiet and calm as always, and they took heart. When Marion walked past them on the narrow gun platform, inside the walls, they tried to grin at him. Marion smiled back, not saying very much. One of these boys was his nephew, Gabriel Marion, for whom he had a deep affection he seldom tried to express. Others were among the men he had recruited in Georgetown and along the Great Pee Dee and the Black River, almost exactly a year ago. He had trained them to march straight, to handle their guns, to obey the commands of the drill. He hadn't known how to teach them courage for the hours that lay ahead. He looked at them and nodded, and somehow they felt braver. They were able to grin almost naturally at the sound of Peter Horry's stuttering orders. Captain Horry always stuttered a little when he was excited.

Suddenly the British ships were bearing down upon them, sails limp in the sultry, almost windless morning, but carried forward by a strong flood tide. Their gun ports were huge and so numerous that it was hard to count them. But the men already knew their guns totaled two hundred seventy—nearly ten times the number of their own. And one of the vessels was a bomb ship, ominously named the *Thunder*. She could throw thirteen-inch shells which might explode the Patriots' scant supply of ammunition high into the hot blue sky.

The ships moved fast, with the *Thunder* in the lead supported by the twenty-two gun *Friendship*. Within minutes—or so it seemed to the breathless men inside the little fort—seven men-of-war had passed the *Thunder* and grouped themselves into formation. The *Active* dropped anchor only four hundred yards from the fort. The six others lined up behind her in two parallel rows.

"Fire!" Moultrie bellowed.

"Fire!" Marion's voice echoed from the left wing of the fort where he commanded.

Not more than twenty-five of the Patriots' guns could be brought to bear on the enemy, but they made a magnificent din as they boomed out into the morning sunshine.

Then, through the smoke, the *Active* showed her broadside, and all her starboard guns let loose in one long, terrible bombardment. The thick, sand-filled walls of little Fort Sullivan shook to their foundations. The air was filled with flying sand and debris and deafening, terrifying noise.

After that it was difficult to keep track of what happened. One of the *Thunder's* bombs fell into the powder magazine and only swift orders and swift execution doused it with sand before it exploded. Brilliant British marksmanship sank ball after ball into the walls, and the men on the platforms grabbed at each other to keep their feet in the shock of the concussions. But the spongy palmetto logs absorbed the cannon balls and closed around them. And through all the confusion, the noise, the smoke and the choking dust, the Patriots kept their own biggest guns trained on the two fifty-gun ships, the *Experiment* and the flagship *Bristol*. On the latter's deck stood Sir Peter Parker, commander of the fleet. Commanding the *Bristol* below was Lord William Campbell, royal governor of South Carolina, a volunteer on this expedition against the city that had briefly been his home.

Suddenly a sharp eye, squinted against the smoke, saw that the *Bristol's* cable had been shot away and that she was turning end onto the fort, all her fifty guns useless. The Patriots raked her then, fore and aft. Her captain's arm was torn off. Sir Peter was wounded twice. The jagged splinter that penetrated Lord William's side killed him a few days later.

Marion himself aimed most of the guns on his platform, so that not a shot would be wasted by inexperienced marksmen. But the Patriot crews were working fast, loading, ramming and firing with a speed remarkable in unseasoned men. Whenever the smoke lighted for a moment they could see the results of their work. Triumphant in the knowledge that they were doing serious damage to the British fleet, they forgot the scantiness of the fort's ammunition supply. They were sternly reminded of it about noon, when a messenger got through from the city bringing an order from Lee. Moultrie was commanded to spike the fort's guns and abandon post as soon as his ammunition was exhausted.

Moultrie glowered. "Then we won't exhaust it," he declared.

"Slow your fire, men." The word went along the platform. "When the ammunition goes, we go too. Easy, now—easy!"

Somehow the men obeyed, holding their hands steady, waiting long, agonizing moments between bursts—when they knew each moment might be their last. The roaring guns of the ships seemed to sound with louder and fiercer intensity, now that the answering fire from the fort had slackened. It was a terrible and helpless feeling for a man to stand motionless beside a long black barrel that was growing cool to the touch, to know that he dared not reply to the deadly balls spurting from those gaping portholes.

Shortly after noon the British began the maneuver Lee had predicted. The three ships in the second line of the formation hauled up their anchors and started to move past the fort. Their obvious intention was to enter the cove behind it, cutting the fort off from the mainland and attacking its vulnerable rear.

But now good fortune lent its hand to the outnumbered, outgunned Patriots. Two of the moving ships ran afoul of each other and in a few moments all three were stuck fast on a shoal. One lost her bowsprit under a few well-aimed shots from the fort. Two freed themselves eventually, but only one later rejoined the battle line.

The *Thunder* was the next to fall from the enemy's ranks. The recoil of her big mortars, overcharged to increase their range, had damaged her so severely that she was no longer fit for service. Of the fifty-some shells she had sent into the fort, scarcely one had done any noticeable harm.

By early afternoon the Americans were lightheaded with the knowledge that they had held off a fleet of the greatest navy in the world for several long hours. But by then too their ammunition was dwindling fast, and six ships still stood in front of them pouring a steady rain of fire at their walls.

Moultrie gave orders that his men should fire only once every ten minutes. Still the precious pile of shot diminished. Then word reached the fort that the British force on Long Island had already landed on Sullivan's Island, and Moultrie slowed his fire almost to a standstill to preserve his tiny remaining store of shot and powder for the attack he now expected from the rear. He had sent a desperate message to President Rutledge asking for more supplies, but they had not arrived yet—might not arrive at all.

That was when Major Marion left the island in a small boat, with a few men, and managed somehow to reach the armed American vessel lying in a creek close to the city. He took all the powder he found aboard her and brought it back to the fort. It was not very much, but it was enough to support a show of fire for some time. Just before it gave out, the hoped-for supplies from President Rutledge arrived. With them was a note to Moultrie scribbled hastily on a scrap of paper:

Dear Sir:
   I send you 500 pounds of powder ... You know our collection is not very great. HONOR and VICTORY, my good sir, to you and our worthy countrymen with you.
                                                    Yours,
                                                    J. Rutledge
   P.S. Do not make too free with your cannon. Cool and do mischief.

The men at the fort liked the message from their president, but they scarcely needed it. Lee found them so cool when he visited the fort, shortly afterward, that he said, "I see you are doing very well here—you have no occasion for me." The words must have cost a good deal to the man who had planned to remove Moultrie from his command that very day. But Lee had never doubted Moultrie's courage, and now he knew that Moultrie and Marion could also command courage from their men.

About seven o'clock, when the sun was setting, the fire on both sides slowed down. By nine-thirty it ceased altogether, with a final shot which tradition says Marion fired, an amazing one that plunged into the *Bristol's* cabin, killed two officers there and then burst on through the deck beyond where it killed three seamen. At eleven o'clock the battered British ships slipped their cables and rode the last of the ebb tide to a safe anchorage a league from the fort.

A hundred men on the *Bristol* had been killed or wounded. There were nine shots in her mainmast and seven in her mizzenmast. The fifty-gun *Experiment* was scarcely better off and had lost as many men. The *Solebay* had lost twelve men, the *Active* seven. The captain of the *Acteon* scuttled his ship. During that long bloody day the Patriots had fired less than five thousand pounds of powder, but they had crippled a whole fleet and killed over two hundred seamen and officers.

The British had used more than seven times that much powder and had succeeded in killing or wounding only thirty-seven of little Fort Sullivan's defenders.

Word soon came to the fort that it had witnessed the only action of the day. The British land forces on Long Island had not even attempted the attack Moultrie had expected—had even mistakenly thought to be in progress during the afternoon. Sir Henry Clinton, in command there, later explained his inaction by saying the waters in the inlet had suddenly risen to a depth too great to be forded. In England he was laughed at for the excuse. One wit, writing in an antigovernment paper, referred to the biblical miracle of the Red Sea, washed back to permit the Hebrews safe passage, and added that on Sullivan's Island

> The miracle reversed is still as great—
> From two feet deep the water rose to seven.

As for the Carolinians, they didn't ridicule their enemy. They knew the extent of the courage and skill that had saved them, and gave thanks for the fortunate wind that had run three British ships aground at a crucial moment of the day. President Rutledge visited the island, with an admiring crowd of ladies and gentlemen from the city, to give the men his personal thanks. Lee made handsome if grudging amends for his earlier mistrust.

"I do most heartily thank you all and shall do you justice in my letters to Congress," he wrote to Moultrie. "I have applied for some rum for your men. They deserve every comfort that can be afforded them!" To Rutledge he admitted—and Rutledge took care to let Moultrie and Marion and the rest see the letter —that "Their conduct is such as does them the greatest honor. No men ever did, and it is impossible ever can, behave better."

No Patriot in South Carolina would have disagreed with him. Charleston had been saved, and Moultrie and Marion and their men were the city's heroes.

CHAPTER

VI

The Battle of Sullivan's Island was the first real American victory of the Revolution. The second and equally important one, if not so dramatically swift, was the triumph of Carolina Patriots over the Tory-led Indians who began to ravage the Up Country at the same time the British ships launched their attack against Charleston. That uprising developed into a bloody struggle that lasted well into the autumn, but finally the Cherokees sued for peace and the Patriots seemed to have control of all of Carolina.

These two victories provided the best, almost the only, good news American Patriots heard during the second half of 1776 and most of 1777. In those same eighteen months, up North, Washington's ragged and ill-organized army was beaten on Long Island in the colony of New York, pushed out of New York City and retreated miserably all the way across New Jersey into Pennsylvania, always just a little ahead of Lord Howe's pursuing redcoats. Everywhere in the middle colonies Tories and neutrals were eagerly pledging or repledging their loyalty to the King. If Patriots had not been able to remind themselves of that decisive victory on Sullivan's Island, they would have had little reason to hope that Americans could ever withstand the might of Britain. Even the soldiers with Washington, seldom respectful of their officers, cheered Charles Lee whenever he appeared among them, because they thought he was responsible for that victory. Many of them thought Lee should be given Washington's post as commander-in-chief.

But in Charleston, of course, it was Moultrie and his men who were recognized as the city's saviors. The little fort on Sullivan's Island was named Fort Moultrie in honor of their gallant stand there. And the excitement of the victory carried the most timid rebel into the camp of those who spoke up loudly in favor of the Declaration of Independence, when news of that Declaration reached the colony in August of 1776. Had the news arrived earlier, most Carolinians would probably have found the document too rash and dangerous. Their delegates to the Continental Congress, in fact, had signed it only to show that Carolina stood united with the rest of the colonies, and afterwards were afraid to let their friends at home know what they had done. But Marion and his fellow delegates to the Carolina Congress, called together in September to consider the document, declared that it was "not only justifiable, but absolutely unavoidable," and pledged themselves "at every hazard to maintain it, so that after we have departed our children and their latest posterity may have cause to bless our memory."

Marion attended that meeting with new insignia on his old blue uniform, insignia that symbolized further unity among the colonies. Each had been asked to supply a specific number of regiments to the Continental Army, and on the day before the Congress met Carolina had filled her quota of six by transferring all her provincial regiments—Marion's Second and the other five already recruited—to Washington's command. They all became part of what was called the Southern Army of the Continental Establishment.

A few weeks later Moultrie was promoted to brigadier general, Lieutenant Colonel Motte became colonel of the Second Regiment in his place and Marion became lieutenant colonel. When Motte resigned in 1778 Marion himself would become the regiment's commander. He didn't become a full colonel at the same time, but there was a reason for that. Prisoner exchanges were conducted by rank—a sergeant for a sergeant, a colonel for a colonel—and there were very few full colonels in the British army, whose regimental commanders were known as lieutenant colonels instead. So by 1778 the Americans had begun to call their own regimental commanders by that title too, in order that one who was captured could be exchanged as soon as the Americans had captured the head of a British regiment.

Marion's duties as a legislator had grown heavier, because there were so many problems for Carolina's new young government to settle. But as the years 1777, 1778 and 1779 dragged by, Lieutenant Colonel Marion wasn't always able to be present at the sessions of Congress. The Southern Army was frequently on the march during that period, and its officers often on active duty.

It was true that Charleston had already been saved. But the glory of that victory over Sir Peter Parker's fleet soon gave way to a grim realization that England was still determined to win for herself the wealth and allegiance of the South. Sir Peter's defeat had simply caused her to change the direction of her attack. By the beginning of the new year, 1777, she was making raids to the north from bases in Florida, whose population still remained loyal to the King. Her immediate intention was to conquer Georgia, weakest of the Southern colonies, and her first principal target was its chief city, Savannah, which lay just across the Savannah River from South Carolina.

Once, early in 1777, Marion hurried south with six hundred men when news reached Charleston that Savannah was in danger. That time the enemy retreated and Marion brought his troops back home again. But late in 1778 Marion was again hastening southward toward the threatened city.

On that occasion both he and Moultrie were under the personal orders of General Benjamin Lincoln, newly appointed commander of the Southern Army. Leader of the rebellious Massachusetts militia at the beginning of the war, Lincoln had risen quickly in the Continental ranks. Now Washington and the whole Patriot South looked to him to drive the British out of Georgia.

Lincoln had brought south with him only General Casimir Pulaski, the Polish nobleman who had volunteered in the rebel cause, and the remnants of Pulaski's brigade, which had recently suffered a severe defeat in New Jersey. But twelve hundred men were rounded up, with great labor, to serve under his command, and it was this sizable force of Continentals and militia that Lincoln led toward Savannah three days after Christmas in the year 1778.

At the little village of Purysburgh, on the South Carolina side of the Savannah River, Lincoln came to an abrupt halt. News had just reached him that Augustine Prevost, the British general, had already conquered Savannah and was sending his victorious troops inland to consolidate his hold on all of Georgia. The news meant that South Carolina, separated from Georgia only by a river, had suddenly become the Patriots' southern frontier.

From that time forward, throughout the early months of 1779, the Americans under Lincoln played a sort of cat-and-mouse game with the British, moving back and forth along the Savannah River. Having divided his force into two main bodies, Lincoln took one under his own direction to harry the enemy inland in the neighborhood of Augusta. The other, under Moultrie—Marion remained with him—sent out raiding parties from the Purysburgh camp, about fifteen miles from the coast. But the American forces lacked sufficient ammunition and supplies. Their ranks were soon thinned by desertions and illness and disrupted by militiamen who objected to serving under a Continental officer. Neither group was strong enough to seek out a large British force and engage it in open combat.

Charleston grew more and more seriously alarmed. Even Moultrie, usually so confident, sent no comforting words to his friends there. He could only advise them to keep the roads into town in good repair, so that he and Lincoln and the men serving with them could reach Charleston quickly if the British decided to march on the city. But he sent something better than words. He sent Marion back to the city to reinforce Fort Moultrie.

Once back in Charleston, however, in mid-April, Marion realized that it was the city's land defenses that would be the most likely object of assault. Breastworks and trenches were already being built, running behind the city from the Ashley River across the peninsula to the Cooper, but a vast amount of work still remained to be done and the news from the field grew daily worse.

By the end of the month Moultrie was driven out of Purysburgh and had retreated to Coosawhatchie, fifteen miles closer to Charleston. A few days later, on May 5, he had to retreat again, to Ashepoo. This settlement was scarcely forty miles from Charleston, and the British under Prevost were still at his heels.

"We are greatly too few to make head against them," Moultrie wrote frankly to Charleston. Nearly half his force had left him within the past day, he added. They had hurried ahead to look after families and property in the enemy's path, which he himself found "very natural." But he feared that civilians and soldiers both would soon be flooding into Charleston at a rapid pace, and warned his friends to be prepared to look after them all, as well as to defend the city. "Get all the rice you can in store," he advised. "For God's sake, let us not want provision; have your work round the town finished as fast as possible; as the enemy march very rapidly, have a number of large cannon mounted on your lines."

The next day, May 6, Moultrie was still closer to Charleston, and the enemy—he estimated their number at three thousand—continued to follow just behind him. Riding furiously, he reached the city the following day.

Alongside him, as he tore breathlessly down the last few miles of the peninsula, hurried militiamen who had ignored earlier appeals for aid but who were now hastening to Charleston's defense. Traveling in the other direction, and numerous enough to clog the road, were families seeking safety outside the city and soldiers leaving their posts to guard their homes in the country against the oncoming British. The city itself, when Moultrie reached it, was in a turmoil. There seemed reason enough for panic in the scant numbers of armed men, including even the untrained militia, who were actually on hand and willing to remain to face an enemy.

The depleted force Moultrie had brought with him numbered only a few hundred men. Most of Carolina's Continental regiments, plus other units now totaling an impressive four thousand, were with Lincoln—and Lincoln was near Augusta almost one hundred and fifty miles away. Urgent letters had already gone out imploring his quick march to Charleston, but no one knew whether he could reach there before the British arrived. No one could even be sure he had received the letters.

Nevertheless Moultrie and his staff stubbornly readied the small forces at their command and spaced them out along the new redoubts guarding the city. Each man was issued a hundred rounds of ammunition. Empty hogsheads were provided for water in the trenches so that, as Moultrie pointed out, no frightened militiaman seeking an excuse to leave the lines could plead the "pretense" of thirst. Marion took charge of the left redoubt, with only a hundred of his own regiment to support him. The rest, with General Pulaski's handful of infantry, occupied a half-moon entrenchment just behind the redoubts, to serve as scouts and reserves.

On the morning of May 11 the enemy crossed the Ashley River, at a point twelve miles above Charleston, and marched straight down the peninsula toward the city at its tip. General Pulaski, with a few hundred men, rode out to engage them, and found himself immediately caught up in so fierce a skirmish that he lost most of his infantry within a few minutes. He was barely able to bring the few survivors back to the safety of the redoubts.

After that the British came on unmolested until they were within a mile of the lines. The Patriots stopped them there by firing the big cannon at their city gates. For the rest of the afternoon General Prevost and his redcoats and Hessian troops remained where they were, apparently waiting for darkness in order to advance closer.

Slowly the hours went by. Marion moved quietly among his men, some of whom had been with him at the Sullivan's Island battle. They had faced danger before—had even, as now, faced an enemy far stronger than themselves. They were standing firmly to their posts, guns ready, eyes and ears alert.

Not all the troops were so calm. Some had never been under fire and were terrified. Others, if less frightened, were still miserably sure that the small American force could never prevent the British from overwhelming the city. Even President Rutledge came to that conclusion during the long hours of the night. He had heard reports of British brutality in Georgia, and it seemed to him that the people of Charleston, huddled now behind the locked doors of their homes, might soon be the victims of that same brutality. At three o'clock in the morning he called his military and civilian leaders into council to suggest that they parley with the enemy.

Moultrie, characteristically, was opposed to the suggestion, and said that he himself was unwilling to send a flag of truce to Prevost. But Rutledge persisted. Perhaps he hoped that a parley would at best win them a delay, during which Lincoln might arrive. Finally Moultrie was persuaded to ask Prevost on what terms he would be "disposed to grant a capitulation," if Moultrie himself were "inclined to capitulate."

By eleven o'clock that morning the reply came back. General Prevost declared himself eager to prevent "the evils and horrors attending the event of a storm (which cannot fail to be successful)" and would accept capitulation if the city's inhabitants "who may not choose to receive the generous offers of peace and protection, may be received as prisoners of war."

Again the Patriots conferred, decided that they could not accept "so dishonorable a proposal," and suggested a discussion between officers of both sides to settle upon other terms. Prevost scorned the suggestion. A little later he scorned the Patriots' next reluctantly delivered message, offering to submit if Carolina might be considered as neutral until the end of the war, when her status would be determined by the treaty of peace. Prevost would accept no terms except complete surrender. Since the Charleston garrison was in arms, he pointed out, he could regard its defenders as nothing but prisoners of war.

Moultrie and Rutledge and the rest of the council met for the last time, desperately aware of the grave decision they faced. For some weeks now pessimistic folk had been declaring that if Charleston were lost, the North would make no attempt to recapture her. Many Northerners, they declared, were ready to abandon the whole South permanently to the enemy, in the hope of saving their own skins. Was Charleston now going to be lost —and without a fight? And if she were lost, and all her men-in-arms made prisoners of war, what hope could there be for the future?

"The point is this," Moultrie put it to the council members briefly, "am I to deliver you up prisoners of war or not?"

There were murmurings among them, but no decisive voice could be heard until Moultrie himself spoke again. "I am determined not to deliver you up as prisoners of war," he announced. "We will fight it out."

"Thank God! We are upon our legs again!" one officer cried.

And having flown the flag that spelled their refusal to accept Prevost's ultimatum, they prepared for battle.

But by then it was late in the afternoon. Neither side took any action for the rest of that day. Again darkness fell and again a long night wore slowly by.

"They're gone!" The incredulous Patriot shout that roused the weary troops at the first light of dawn brought every man straight up and staring wildly toward the British encampment. "The British are gone!"

For a time they could hardly believe it was true. When they did finally believe it—after General Pulaski rode a swift circuit of the British lines and found them completely deserted—they still couldn't understand what had happened. Later they learned that the British had intercepted a letter from General Lincoln in which he said, "we are making, and shall continue to make, every exertion for the relief of Charleston. The baggage will be left . . . Our men are full of spirits . . . Do not give up, or suffer the people to despair."

The sense of wild rejoicing that had seized Charleston by that time, however, could not be sobered by thoughtful considerations of that letter, and the effect it must have had upon the enemy. People preferred not to stop and think too seriously about Prevost's situation, about the fact that he had after all had only some three thousand men—not a very large force if he expected to be squeezed between Lincoln's oncoming troops and the Charleston redoubts. It was pleasanter to believe that Charleston had once again been saved because her Patriots were courageous, because her defenders, few as they might be, had the gallantry to face the British without flinching.

But men with some experience of warfare—and by now Marion was one of these—knew only too well that the British were still as great a menace to the city as they had been before their sudden departure. The only question was how soon, and with what strength, the enemy would strike again.

CHAPTER

VII

General Lincoln, reaching Charleston a few days after the British had so silently slipped away, learned almost immediately that Prevost had not gone very far. The cautious British general had simply moved in a half-circle around the town, to the south and east, and established himself on one of the islands that fringe the Carolina coast—John's Island, separated from James Island, where Fort Johnson stood, by an inlet called Wappoo Cut. He was far too close to Charleston for comfort, in Lincoln's opinion, and Lincoln decided to take the initiative. His hope was to destroy Prevost's force, or drive it out of the state, before it could receive reinforcements and launch another attack.

Marion apparently resumed the post that had been entrusted to him before, as commander of Fort Moultrie, while Lincoln and Moultrie planned a two-prong attack on John's Island. Lincoln was to approach with one force by land; Moultrie was to bring a second force by boat across Wappoo Cut. But Moultrie failed to have his boats ready in time, and the attack failed. The British did withdraw from the island not long afterward, but only to move a little farther south, from island to island along the coast, burning homes and stealing horses and food and slaves as they went. At Beaufort they stopped and entrenched themselves again.

Lincoln, still determined to drive them completely out of Carolina, marched southward in their wake, but by an inland route, and set up a camp at Sheldon, fifteen miles from the enemy. There he ordered Marion to join him, in the hope that the quiet little Second Regiment commander could once more work his miracle of disciplining weary troops and militia into a fighting force. But not even Marion could train men who didn't exist, and as the summer drifted into autumn the troops under Lincoln seemed to melt away.

Marion understood why the camp grew emptier each day. The war had already been going on for more than three years, and it seemed to have reached a stalemate that many people thought might last forever. They were tired of fighting, tired even of victories over an enemy that always seemed to rise up again stronger than before. Men in the Continental regiments were simply refusing to re-enlist when their two-year terms were over, and new recruits were hard to find.

Militiamen were also scarce, although a plan worked out some time before was designed to keep one-third of the entire militia in arms at all time, each third to serve for a period of three months. The plan had looked excellent on paper. But some men disappeared into the back country rather than submit to the draft when they were called up. Others, with Tory sympathies, submitted under pressure and deserted to the better-fed, better-uniformed British at the first opportunity. Even those who reported in good faith could seldom be persuaded to extend their service past the last day of the third month, whether or not a replacement was available.

Of course Carolina was not alone in this situation. Washington was complaining bitterly, month after month, that he could not keep an adequate fighting force of regular troops in the field, and could not depend on state militias for real support in his campaigns. But with an enemy actually inside her borders, and with little or no help to be expected from the North, or from America's newly won ally, France, Carolina was in a particularly serious plight.

Then, suddenly, as if by magic, new hope was born. Marion was in Charleston, attending a session of the legislature, when

President Rutledge announced the astounding news: a French fleet had just arrived off Charleston, ready to join Lincoln in a land-and-sea assault upon British-held Savannah.

The legislature hastily adjourned. The city feted the flamboyant fleet commander, Charles Estaing, usually known by his title of Count d'Estaing. Marion and the other officers rejoined their regiments. Almost overnight those regiments swelled with men convinced that now, at last, the British would really be defeated. Even the militia flocked eagerly to the ranks.

Lincoln wasted no time when the forces under his command, including now some Georgia Patriots, rose to four thousand. He knew that d'Estaing had three thousand French troops aboard his ships, and that the two allied forces together nearly tripled the number of British reported to be stationed in Savannah. Leaving Moultrie in command at Charleston, he started to march south in mid-September. Marion and the Second Regiment were with him.

Patriots confidently assured each other, as they swung jubilantly down dusty country lanes, that when they and the French simultaneously arrived at Savannah—the Patriots by land, the French by sea—the British would surrender the city without firing a gun in its defense.

But the Battle of Savannah proved to be a bloody affair.

Count d'Estaing, arriving there first, found that a bar prevented his large ships from coming close enough to shore to take part in an attack. So he disembarked his men in small boats some miles south of the city and, without waiting for Lincoln's forces to join him, marched immediately forward. A messenger he sent ahead, carried to Prevost, the British commander, an arrogant demand for surrender in the name of the French king.

Prevost requested twenty-four hours in which to consider his answer and the possible terms of surrender. D'Estaing airily agreed.

Prevost put the time to good use. He spent it fortifying the city and bringing in eight hundred veterans from his Beaufort garrison. At the end of the twenty-four hours—Lincoln and his men were just arriving at the rear of the town—Prevost gave his reply. He was ready to defend the town to the last extremity.

Horry reported later, according to the biographer Weems, that he had never before seen Marion so outraged as when he realized the difficult and unnecessary task that now faced the comparatively raw American troops.

"Who ever heard of anything like this before?" Marion demanded. "First allow an enemy to entrench, and then fight him!"

But now there was nothing else to be done. The British, protected on the north by the Savannah River and on the west by a swampy morass, had already started to build defenses on the level ground to the east and south of the city. They were raising three strong redoubts on their right, close to the swamp, and two on their left near the river. The dozen guns on their fortifications when d'Estaing first appeared increased day by day until they numbered a hundred.

Lincoln set his men to building approaches to those lines, and bringing guns up from the ships. It was a slow business, carried out under constant danger. Two weeks went by before the Patriots could mount their guns and mortars within range of the enemy. Finally, on October 4, the French and American allies opened fire.

The cannonade continued for five days. It was doing very little damage to the town, as it happened, but besieged Savannah was expected to surrender when her supplies ran out and her population, civilian and military both, faced starvation.

D'Estaing grew impatient. The one success he had achieved previously, the seizure of two British Caribbean islands, had been accomplished with dramatic speed. This static kind of siege warfare was too unexciting for his taste. He told Lincoln that he would withdraw his forces unless Savannah was assaulted immediately. He wanted the allied troops to undertake the very task Marion had dreaded on their behalf—to hurl themselves against those sturdy fortifications which Prevost now had bristling with guns and manned by experienced men. Lincoln could do nothing but agree to the Frenchman's demand.

The best of Prevost's forces were stationed in the three redoubts on his right, close to the swamp. Among them was a regiment of South Carolina Tories. Marion's Second Regiment of South Carolina Patriots was in the body of troops, led by Lincoln and d'Estaing themselves, scheduled to assault those three enemy strongholds.

Marion couldn't guess that this would be the Second Regiment's last battle under his command. Looking over the ranks as they stood quietly awaiting the order to march, he was probably thinking only of the men themselves, and wondering how many would come safely through the day ahead. They were pale, some of them, but confident as always in his presence.

It was one o'clock in the morning, on October 9, 1779, when the order came to move forward. Silently the ranks marched out of camp, leaving only the invalids behind to tend the fires. Each man had forty rounds of cartridges and a spare flint in his pocket.

One column headed toward the river, to attack the enemy's two left redoubts. The second moved in the opposite direction. Part of it was to go toward the swamp and a possible route around behind the lines. The rest, including the Second, was to head straight for those three principal redoubts, of which the one called Spring Hill was to be the chief target. Marion's men were to be in the forefront of the attack upon Spring Hill.

Not everything that happened in the next few hours was clear at the time. Marion himself learned part of the story of the battle only after it was over. But two of the major catastrophies of the day occurred almost immediately.

A flooded rice field delayed the party moving toward the river. Daylight found the men still emerging from it and so exposed to a sharp fusillade of enemy fire that they retreated at once.

The line heading toward the swamp lost its way at the edge of the dangerous morass, and in the first light of the rising sun it too was so battered by British guns that it was never able to form its lines.

But Marion's Regiment and the men with them managed to arrive close to their objective before the darkness faded. They were within range of enemy musketry, and the instant their shadowy figures were recognized as targets, those muskets blazed down upon them. They had scarcely fired their own guns for the first time when a heavy crossfire burst at them from the adjoining battery. It was so severe that it destroyed whole ranks of the advancing column at a single barrage. Yet the column didn't waver. Men moved up to take the place of those who had fallen, and it continued forward as a steady pace until it reached the very foot of the redoubt.

There, in the ditch, the fighting was fiercer still. The rattle of guns was constant, and flashing bayonets caught the beams of early morning sunlight.

But the Patriots surged on forward, up the sloping walls under the fire pouring down upon them from above. The British were fighting magnificently, and they had the advantage of position, but the Patriots were successful in the first stage of their assault. A flag of Marion's Regiment was stuck into the earthworks on top of the parapet to mark that Patriot triumph.

The Tories on Spring Hill redoubt were as determined as their fellow Carolinians who were now their enemies, and Prevost was ready with reserves. The fresh grenadiers and marines he sent against the already-weary assault force were able to prevent the Patriots on the top of the parapet from turning and spreading along it. Some of the assaulters were instantly hurled back into the ditch. There, lying helpless on the bodies of their dead and wounded friends, they were mercileslsy slaughtered by the men who swept down the walls after them. The rest, fighting under ceaseless fire, were driven more slowly but just as inevitably back down the slope they had so laboriously climbed.

The whole battle lasted a little less than an hour. Once the Americans were forced from their most forward position they were given no opportunity to regain it. General Pulaski, galloping headlong between the redoubts in an attempt to get behind the enemy lines for a last desperate attack, was shot down in the midst of his charge. Lincoln and d'Estaing withdrew their troops then, unable even to bring their casualities off the field when they left it in full retreat.

Back at the camp that afternoon, Marion's staff, staggeringly reduced within a few hours, gathered beneath the smoke-stained regimental flag that had been retrieved from the parapet where it waved so briefly. Marion had lost his major, a man with whom he had served since the beginning of the war; they had been elected to their captaincies the same day. He had lost three of his lieutenants. He had lost men from the ranks whose names he knew well, and others whose names he had scarcely had time to learn. He knew they had all died in vain.

The Patriot camp outside of Savannah was a place of deathly quiet during the next few days. Briefly Lincoln considered continuing his siege of the city—the siege d'Estaing had interrupted with his insistence upon assault. But d'Estaing was opposed and Lincoln was again forced to accept his decision. Shortly afterward d'Estaing reembarked his men and sailed away from the coast, only to run into a storm that scattered his ships so completely they could no longer be useful to the Patriot cause. Lincoln called in his own officers and issued orders for the march home.

There could be no doubt that the Second Regiment had, as General Moultrie said, "gained great honor" at the Spring Hill redoubt. Certainly it had shown magnificent and disciplined courage. But in Marion's judgment—and there was time for a man to sort out his ideas on the miserable march northward, past fields the British had destroyed and farmhouses they had burned to the ground—courage alone was not enough. The battle of Savannah had been lost because it was fought too late to catch the enemy unprepared, too early to take advantage of the lines the Patriots had been building. But partly, too, it had been lost because the British had such staunch Tory aid. Perhaps more than once that day a Tory had aimed his gun at a Patriot brother's head, and a Patriot had lunged with his bayonet at a Tory cousin's heart. The war the Patriots' had begun in the hope of winning their rights from a "wicked ministry" in London had become a bitter civil war. Savannah and all Georgia had been that war's first victim in the South. Charleston and South Carolina were likely to be the next. And the prospect of an open civil war in Carolina was one Marion at least could not visualize without horror and dread.

When the weary and depleted Patriot companies reached the encampment at Sheldon, that post inland from Beaufort where Lincoln had stationed himself some time before, Lincoln left Marion there in command of most of the forces. Marion's assignment was to prevent Prevost from crossing the Savannah River and obtaining supplies from already-ravaged South Carolina farms.

But Marion had been at Sheldon only a short time when dispatches informed him that the expected attack on Charleston would probably take place in the near future. News confirming that possibility was trickling down from the North almost every day, and the situation in the North itself was one reason why the news was almost certain to be reliable.

Conditions there had changed since those days in 1776 and early 1777, when Washington's Patriots were retreating constantly through New York and New Jersey and letting the British take Philadelphia. The defeat of General John Burgoyne at Saratoga in late '77, and the capture of his army, had given the Patriots the upper hand in the territory north of New York. The British had evacuated Philadelphia and marched back to New York, this time with Washington as the pursuer. The British still held that city, and Washington wasn't strong enough to attack them there, but the British didn't dare venture out of New York past the Patriot forces in order to attempt another march southward.

It was for that reason that the British had decided to take part of their cooped-up New York troops, strengthen them with reinforcements from New England, and transport them south by water for a full-scale attack upon Charleston. Twice before they had decided that the best strategy was to defeat the South first, and use it as a base—and its loyal Tories as allies—for a campaign against the North. Both times they had failed to take the South's richest and most important city. Every Patriot could take for granted that they had no intention of failing a third time.

In the late fall of 1779, therefore, Charleston began to prepare itself for this third attack. All signs pointed to the fact that it would be far worse than the two it had already survived. Now Charleston had to anticipate a simultaneous assault by land and by sea, and it could hardly hope to be saved again as it had twice been saved in the past, once by a fortunate wind and next by an enemy decision to retreat rather than fight.

It is true that Sir Henry Clinton, the British commander-in-chief now busy in New York organizing his Charleston expedition, was the same man who had been ridiculed for failing to ford the little inlet between Long and Sullivan's Islands, on the day the fort there was under fire. But that was far in the past, and Sir Henry was now a more experienced and more determined foe. He had worked out a plan that couldn't be upset by a suddenly swollen ford. The plan would take time to put into practice, but Sir Henry was ready to give it all the time it required.

Once more Charleston Patriots found themselves preparing and enlarging the breastworks that stretched from the Ashley to the Cooper rivers—the ditched-based wall that transformed the tip of the peninsula into a fortress, surrounded by water on its other three sides. Once more they prepared to mount cannon along their wharves and to strengthen Fort Moultrie and Fort Johnson. They laid in supplies and ammunition. They instructed householders—those who didn't leave the city at the first sign of danger—in the best methods for fighting fires and protecting their homes with sandbags and cobblestones ripped up out of the streets.

In the meantime Marion and Moultrie set up a new camp near Dorchester for the purpose of rounding up any boats, cattle and other supplies that might otherwise fall into enemy hands. When that job was done both were ordered into the city. Lincoln was calling in almost every man available, with the exception of a small party of horses under General Isaac Huger, assigned to keep open the line of communication between Charleston and the strategic point of Monck's Corner, at the head of the Cooper River. Even so his defensive force in the city—including the eight hundred men still left in the Carolina regiments and every militiaman who could be pressed into service—numbered only a little over six thousand.

On February 11, 1780, Sir Henry Clinton landed on John's Island, thirty miles south of Charleston. There he was soon joined by reinforcements that brought his troops up to a total of thirteen thousand. Deliberately and cautiously he began to establish one post after another on the south and southeast of the city, always maintaining his communications with the British fleet that was by then blockading the harbor—and that was so powerful that it discouraged any attack by the few American ships collected there. And while Sir Henry proceeded with his careful plan, a party of rangers under the brutal Lieutenant Colonel Banastre Tarleton surrounded and almost completely destroyed the small group of infantrymen stationed at Monck's Corner. Tarleton's success insured Sir Henry's encirclement of the city. It was a slow process, but every day it came a little closer to completion. Barricaded behind the fortifications of Charleston, the Patriots waited helplessly for his attack.

On March 28 the British crossed the Ashley River, as Prevost had done once before, and started down the narrow peninsula toward Charleston at its tip. Lincoln sent out a few light infantrymen to skirmish with their advance guard, but they did little damage. The British continued to move forward. By the second day of April they were building their own redoubts facing the Patriots' lines. Less than a week later the British fleet sailed past Fort Moultrie, and this time the guns from the little fortress failed to stop their passage. On Monday, the 10th of April, Sir Henry and the vice-admiral in charge of his fleet called upon the city to surrender. Lincoln replied that it was his "duty and inclination" to defend Charleston to the last extremity. Shortly after nine o'clock on Thursday morning, April 12, the bombardment of the city began.

But on one of the evenings before those fateful shots sped up and over the walls of Charleston, several Patriot soldiers and citizens had dinner together in a house on Tradd Street. Marion was among them. All were weary, and tense with the knowledge that the British asasult would soon begin. Their host insisted that they would all be better for a considerable amount of brandy. When he had made them comfortable in his second-floor drawing room, and filled their glasses, he followed the custom of the day by locking the door of the room where they sat. The gesture said, in effect, "I do not expect you to leave until my brandy is gone. It is all yours."

Everyone who knew Francis Marion always spoke of him as a temperate man. Perhaps he drank a little brandy that night. Perhaps he drank none at all. But in any case he apparently felt that Patriot officers needed clear heads just then, and that they ought not to be away from their posts for more than a few hours. The talk was still lively around the table, and their host's brandy not yet nearly exhausted, when Marion decided to leave.

His friends wouldn't let him go. They urged, they pleaded. Half-laughing, half-serious, they stood guard at the locked door. So Marion turned to the long French windows overlooking the garden, stepped through onto the balcony and swung a leg over the railing. He caught himself by one hand for a moment and then let himself drop down.

It was not much of a drop, for so agile a man. But he landed on the cobblestoned carriage drive, and one foot turned under him on a rounded stone. He fell heavily and found he could not stand when he tried to get to his feet. The regimental surgeon, when Marion was carried to his headquarters that night, diagnosed a bad compound fracture of the ankle. Marion, he said, would be incapacitated for weeks.

On the eve of the British bombardment President Rutledge

was persuaded to leave the city, in order to be able to maintain a state government in the event of Charleston's capture. At almost the same time General Lincoln ordered all officers unfit for duty to leave the city too. Marion went because there was nothing else he could do. Feeling like a deserter, and furious at himself for the injury that made him useless at a time when he was desperately needed, he let himself be taken to the plantation home he had scarcely seen for several years.

The British besieged Charleston for a month before Lincoln and his exhausted forces, lacking ammunition, food and even water by then, finally surrendered. The city fell on May 12, 1780. Sir Henry permitted all militia to go home on parole. He held all regular officers and troops as prisoners of war.

England had finally achieved her purpose. She had conquered the South's richest and most important city. She assumed that all Carolina was as good as in her hands—and the number of Tories who quickly pledged allegiance to King George convinced Sir Henry that this assumption was correct. It was then he sent home to England the message that rejoiced his King, the message declaring that "there are few men in South Carolina who are not either our prisoners or in arms with us."

But President Rutledge was neither; he had made his way to safety in North Carolina. General Huger had escaped Tarleton's raiders by hiding all night in a swamp. A man named Thomas Sumter, once commander of Carolina's Sixth Regiment but retired to his plantation in 1777, had also fled north across the border.

And Francis Marion was in hiding in St. John's parish. He was unable to move without help. He had lost his entire regiment; except for those who had been killed during the battle, all its members were being held under guard in Charleston. But he was alive and he was free. The accident he so much regretted had been a fortunate one for the Patriot cause. Francis Marion, onetime commander of the Second Regiment, was about to become Francis Marion, partisan. The most important years of his military career were still ahead of him.

CHAPTER

VIII

For several weeks after the fall of Charleston, Francis Marion lay in hiding in the swamps not far from his home. He didn't dare remain openly at the Pond Bluff house because the British would have found him there. Somehow—probably through his servant, Oscar—he managed to obtain enough food to keep alive. Somehow he learned a good deal about what the British were doing in Charleston and throughout the rest of the state.

Sir Henry Clinton was wasting no time. As soon as he marched into the city he began to put into effect two kinds of measures for making England complete master of all of South Carolina. One required the use of guns and bayonets, the other of promises and threats.

The first measure consisted chiefly of raids on all settlements where any active opposition still showed itself, and of three full-scale forays into the Up Country along routes that fanned out from Charleston like the spokes of a wheel. None of the forces met any real resistance along the way, and the villages at the end meekly accepted the same surrender terms Sir Henry had imposed on Charleston. Each was then fortified to serve as a British stronghold in its own area.

Of course the British redcoats and their Hession and Tory allies were not satisfied simply to march into a village and accept its surrender. They looted as they went. Individual soldiers stole what they could pick up and carry off, and their officers took charge of large-scale operations. They earmarked certain supplies for the use of the army. Other valuable items—silver, slaves, rice and indigo—they sold through their army commissaries and divided the profits according to rank, as naval crews divided spoils taken on the high seas.

One military raid during this period was never forgotten by the people of Carolina. It was conducted by Tarleton's Rangers and earned for him the name of "Butcher" Tarleton. The British officer had heard that there was a small party of about two hundred Virginian Patriots in Carolina. Originally they had been marching toward Charleston to aid in its defense, but had turned back toward home when they heard of the city's capture. Tartleton rode swiftly after them, caught them near the North Carolina line, and brutally massacred or seriously injured almost the entire party. Even when the men threw down their arms in surrender, the slaughter by saber and bayonet continued.

But Sir Henry had another purpose besides the destruction of American Patriots. He wanted to transform some of them into Tories, into allies he could depend on to furnish supplies or serve as recruits for future campaigns. He hoped someday to be able to send a sizable army of American-born Tories northward through North Carolina and Virginia, while he himself held the rebels north of New York, in a grand strategical maneuver that would sever the northern half of the colonies from the southern half and render each more vulnerable to a final assault or an offer of peace. Sir Henry had good reason to think his plan could be worked out. Many Americans were already serving in the British forces. Tarleton's Rangers, for example, had been recruited in New York, and the Spring Hill redoubt at the siege of Savannah had been defended by South Carolina Tories. So it was to win more soldiers of this kind that Sir Henry put into effect his second measure. It consisted at first of promises that sounded honorable and more than generous.

Having welcomed back into the King's protection all men who said they had always been loyal Tories, he promised a full pardon and that same protection to those who had been, as he put it, "misled" into fighting against England. The only price he asked in return was an oath of allegiance to the King. Sir Henry also promised that if South Carolinians proved their loyalty, they would soon be enjoying all their previous rights as British subjects and, in addition, the one further right they had long requested: the right to be taxed only by their own legislature.

But a few weeks later Sir Henry added a threat to those assurances. He said that any Carolinian who did *not* swear allegiance to the King and undertake his duties as a loyal subject—which meant, in effect, volunteering for active service with the British army—would be treated as an enemy; his property would be confiscated and he would be arrested and thrown in jail.

Sir Henry sailed triumphantly back to New York less than a month after he had taken Charleston, leaving Lord Cornwallis and four thousand men behind him to complete the subjection he believed he had already pretty well accomplished.

When Francis Marion heard the first reports that trickled through to him he too must have believed that Sir Henry had thoroughly defeated South Carolina and won her allegiance to the crown.

Many Carolinians, in response to Sir Henry's first promise, had readily sworn their loyalty to the King. Some had always been Tories. Some had always been neutral, not caring which way the war ended but only wanting it to be over. Some had once called themselves Patriots but were now convinced that they had made a mistake and should renew their allegiance to a government willing to treat them so generously. A final group swore allegiance to the King because they had seen the King's armies and had sadly decided that no American army could ever stand up against them. Convinced that South Carolina could never win her own freedom, and that she had been abandoned by the North, they took the oath because they saw no other future for themselves short of imprisonment or exile. From one section alone some four thousand men came forward to take up arms with the redcoats.

But Marion gradually learned that there was another side to the story.

Some people who had thankfully accepted the first offer of pardon were horrified when they discovered they were expected to join in the ranks against fellow Americans, and their gratitude toward the conqueror shriveled into disgust.

Militiamen who had originally been allowed to return home on paroles—which bound them in honor to take no further action in the American cause, but also protected them from being drawn into the British forces—were incensed when Sir Henry declared that every Carolinian had to swear allegiance to the King and defend him with arms. By this declaration Sir Henry was revoking the paroles he himself had given, and many of the men who had accepted those paroles in good faith later deliberately swore oaths of allegiance they had no intention of keeping. They felt that since Sir Henry had backed down on his word, they were free to do the same. They were ready to fight again if they could find the opportunity.

Another group of secret rebels was growing up among men whose property had been destroyed. Patriots who had lost all they owned could see no further reason to cling to the King's protection granted in return for their oaths. They no longer had anything to protect. Many an honest Tory, too, gave up his Tory sympathies when he was robbed by marauders who didn't bother to question his politics once they saw he owned cattle or silver worth stealing.

Still another group of rebels was created by Tarleton's refusal to give quarter to the Virginians he massacred, and by similar brutalities he practiced as he and his Rangers roamed the countryside. Even people who had tried to ignore the war entirely felt hatred for a country that permitted such horrors.

Marion himself had never for a moment considered signing an oath of allegiance. Injured and hunted as he was, it still never occurred to him to come out of hiding and throw in his lot with the British—to whom, of course, he would have been a welcomed and honored ally. He also avoided any foolhardy risks that could have cost him his life, and cost the rebel cause one of the few trained officers left in the South. Coolly and calmly, like the good strategist he had become, he laid his plans to get back into the fight. Some weeks after the fall of Charleston—it was probably early in July—he put those plans into action. His purpose was to travel northward to the North Carolina border, beyond which he knew the Patriot cause was still alive. Somewhere in North Carolina he hoped to find a Continental Army to which he could volunteer his services. President Rutledge was there. Perhaps other South Carolinians had already managed to escape and join him.

Marion had to be lifted onto his horse. His servant, Oscar, seated him in the saddle, got astride another horse himself and was ready to accompany Marion on his journey. There were a few other men with them too, farmers of St. John's parish who felt that if Marion was ready to go on fighting the British, they were ready to stand by him, however black the future looked.

It was an unimpressive little band that started forth one night. Each man had a horse, but he had little else. Probably few of them owned uniforms, but they wouldn't have put them on for this trip in any case; uniforms would be too conspicuous if they were sighted by a British patrol party. They wore their own breeches and jackets or hunting shirts, and small black leather caps. Perhaps Marion had given them the caps, because they were like the ones his men of the Second Regiment had used. They carried small parcels of food, a blanket or two, and whatever weapons they happened to own. They planned to travel chiefly at night, and spend the dangerous hours of daylight hiding in whatever cover the country afforded.

Legend says Marion possessed an almost supernatural ability to find his way through swamps and forests. Certainly he did have an uncanny sense of direction and amazing skill at orienting himself quickly to unfamiliar terrain. But on this trip, as later in his partisan career, he probably made use of other men's knowledge of particular parts of the country, and sought information from known Patriot sympathizers. Refugees had been trickling north for some weeks, and it is possible that a rough route of escape had already been established. Patriots were probably guided along it from one section to another, and warned how to avoid Tories and the British patrols stationed here and there. Perhaps they were even given a little food now and then, but mostly Marion's party had to depend on the country after their own supplies ran out. They could always find wild sweet potatoes, and could shoot small game when they were sure enough of their safety to risk the sound of a shot.

It was not an easy trip. It was not a short one.

Marion heard a horseman behind his party once, as he rode steadily northward. He turned quickly in the saddle, alert for trouble. But a moment later he recognized the man coming toward him. It was Peter Horry. The younger officer's ruddy face lit up when he saw the little colonel. Eagerly Horry helped Oscar lift Marion off his horse—Marion's ankle was "still crazy," Horry remembered long afterward—and as they ate a meager meal beside the trail they pooled what little information they had. Marion knew Horry had been ill at his plantation near Georgetown during the siege of Charleston. Now he learned that Horry had left home because Tarleton had appeared in his neighborhood. Like Marion, Horry was determined to cross the border and enlist with whatever American forces he could find there. When they set off again Horry had become a member of Marion's little party. He remained one of Marion's most devoted followers from that time on.

They had to travel a considerable distance even after they crossed into North Carolina. It wasn't until they reached the little town of Hillsboro, only a few miles south of the Virginia border, that they found the Continental troops they were seeking.

President Rutledge was in Hillsboro. So was General Isaac Huger. So was Johann Kalb, the German-born soldier who had served as a major in the French army and who called himself Baron de Kalb when he crossed the ocean to serve France's New

World ally. Kalb was an able, sensible man, trusted by Washington, who had sent him south not long before to command whatever Continental forces were left in that area.

Kalb welcomed Marion with all the respect due an officer of excellent reputation. He tried to make him comfortable after that pain-wracked journey of several hundred miles, and immediately confirmed Marion's standing with the Continental Army by giving both Horry and Marion appointments to his own staff. The first piece of important news he confided to his new aides was the fact that General Horatio Gates was expected almost any day with a whole army, determined to invade South Carolina and win it back from the British.

It was, of course, remarkably good news to the South Carolinians. After the rumors that Washington and the Continental Congress were ready to abandon the South altogether, Marion had scarcely expected to hear that a sizable American force would soon be attacking Lord Cornwallis. But the news would have been even better if Gates himself had had a better reputation among soldiers. Always vain, Gates had become vainer still when the public heralded him as the hero of the Battle of Saratoga. Men who had been present at that battle, however, gave credit for the victory to other officers. Several of the veteran fighters at the little Hillsboro encampment regretted that Gates would be superseding Kalb and directing all their movements as soon as he appeared among them.

Marion never recorded his own reaction to Gates when that self-satisfied general rode into camp at the head of his forces. But Colonel Otho Williams, a member of Gates' staff and a man who appreciated Marion's skill and experience, recalled the meeting later in these words:

> Col. Marion, a gentleman of South Carolina, had been with the army a few days, attended by a very few followers, distinguished by small leather caps and the wretchedness of their attire; their number did not exceed twenty men and boys, some white, some black and all mounted, but most of them miserably equipped;

their appearance was in fact so burlesque, that it was with much difficulty the diversion of the regular soldiery was restrained by the officers.

It seems unlikely that Gates would have entrusted Marion with any responsible position on his staff. But as it happened a message reached Hillsboro within the next few days which effectively separated the two men. The message came from Williamsburg, a district of South Carolina inland from Georgetown. President Rutledge talked it over with Marion, and Marion agreed without hesitation to do what Rutledge asked him to do: set off for Williamsburg immediately.

The story Marion learned, of what had been going on in that district, has now become part of his own history. It was the beginning of his famous Brigade.

Williamsburg was a large and sparsely settled area bounded roughly by the Santee River on the south and the Pee Dee River on the north. Georgetown was the port for the farmers living there. When the British took over Georgetown they had placed a Captain Ardesoif in charge of the town and all the country around it. Williamsburg was officially under his jurisdiction. But during the early summer of 1780 Ardesoif had not yet had time to extend his authority into that inland section and enforce the demand for oaths of allegiance from all its residents.

Those residents, though largely of Irish descent and inheritors of a violent dislike of British government, for the most part had seen nothing at all of the war up until then, had not volunteered to take any active part in it. But one of them, a Major John James—he was the father of young William Dobein James, author of the sketch of Marion's years as a partisan—had fought under Moultrie and represented Williamsburg in the Provincial Congress. He must have known a good deal about Marion, and Marion must have known him.

Major James took the lead in the events that led up to that message sent to Hillsboro. He was, first of all, active in the public meeting called to discuss the final proclamation issued by Sir Henry Clinton before his departure for New York. As far as the residents of Williambsurg could judge, that proclamation threatened that any man who refused to take up arms against his fellow Americans would be hunted down as an enemy. But it was difficult for them to believe that even England, however ill they thought of her, would expect Americans willingly to kill other Americans. So they had concluded to send a representative to Georgetown to ask the English officer in command there for a precise explanation of Sir Henry's words—words that so flatly contradicted his earlier offer of pardons and paroles. Major James was the representative they chose. He went to Georgetown in the simple clothes of a countryman.

Ardesoif answered James' query with arrogant abruptness. Williamsburg citizens, he said, would have to submit unconditionally to the new proclamation—would have to take up arms for the King as it required. James said, politely, that he didn't think the people he represented would agree to such terms. The British captain flew into a rage. What angered him most was that James dared to speak of himself as representing the people of the district, when Ardesoif himself was in his own opinion the district's only true representative, appointed to that position by the King. Ardesoif threatened James with death at the end of a rope if he used such insolent language again.

James realized he would be utterly helpless if the captain decided to make good his threat. He ran from the house before Ardesoif could summon guards to arrest him, and was pounding down the road on his horse before orders to hold him could be issued.

The people of Williamsburg, when they had heard his report, decided that only one course was open to them. Since they would not take up arms against their fellow Americans, they would have to take up arms against the British instead. With no delay they organized themselves into four companies, each captained by a former militia officer, and sent to Hillsboro the message that Rutledge discussed with Marion. The message asked for an experienced officer to serve as leader of their miniature army.

When Marion left for Williamsburg, late in July, General

Gates was, a staff member said, "glad." The little Second Regiment officer, in his travel-stained clothes, was an embarrassment to the general known for the trappings and glitter of his parade uniforms. But Gates was willing to let even the shabbiest officer do him a service. He ordered Marion, on his way back south, to destroy all the boats, ferries and scows he might encounter at each of the many rivers he would have to cross. Gates was taking for granted that Cornwallis, already known to be marching up from Charleston to meet the American forces, would be routed by Patriot fire and would attempt to flee. Destruction of all boats, Gates thought, would prevent Cornwallis from running so fast that Gates could not administer the thrashing he planned. Gates also ordered Marion to collect all available information about the British forces and forward this intelligence immediately to Gates' headquarters.

Marion carried out the orders to the best of his ability on this difficult trek south again through country now alive with enemy raiding parties and patrols. Peter Horry accompanied him too—Peter's brother, Hugh, a favorite of Marion, would join the group shortly—and so did a handful of other men. They reached Williamsburg on August 12, exactly three months after the fall of Charleston.

Fifteen-year-old William Dobein James later remembered Marion's arrival, and how the men of the district "flocked about him, to obtain a sight of their future commander." In young James' eyes Marion looked "lean and swarthy" in his coarse crimson jacket; he was still limping. But not even pain and weariness could make Marion's eyes other than "black and piercing," and the words *"Liberty or Death"* shone bravely from the little silver crescent he wore on his black leather cap.

Marion too was studying these men he was meeting for the first time. They were not uniformed, and their equipment consisted of whatever muskets or fowling pieces they had been able to collect. They expected no pay for the service they were volunteering. They were aware that once they left the shelter of their own settlements they would have to find their own food or go without. General Gates might have smiled at the idea that they called themselves soldiers, but Marion knew that men who chose to fight of their own free will, and who knew what they were fighting for, were worth ten times their number in handsomely dressed, magnificently equipped, unwillingly drafted recruits.

He didn't make a long speech to tell them that. He had returned to his native state ready to fight the British once more. Now he had a command again, as General Marion of Marion's Brigade—the militia rank he would bear as soon as a new commission from President Rutledge caught up with him. He knew his men understood him without the need for fine words, just as he understood them. Their meeting together proved that they shared one purpose and one goal. It would be useless to talk about it. The time for action had at last arrived.

CHAPTER

IX

Marion led his new Brigade out against the enemy on the second day after his arrival in Williamsburg.

They followed him trustingly. Already they had learned that their leader knew how to guard against surprise. The network of pickets he threw around their camp told them that. Each guard posted along the boundary of the encampment had been taught piercing whistles for signaling the approach of a stranger on foot, on horseback, or traveling by water. And beyond that circle of guards Marion had stationed a second circle of mounted sentinels, chosen for their ability to prowl silently through the woods or to stand motionless for hours if necessary.

The Williamsburg men had also learned that Marion had common sense and ingenuity. Their lack of uniforms didn't trouble him in the least. But their lack of powder and shot, the scarcity of their guns, had prompted him to quick action toward supplying the Brigade with additional weapons of some sort. Almost immediately upon his arrival he had sent scouts out to round up all the saws they could obtain, from farmers and local sawmills. As soon as the first saws were brought in he put volunteer blacksmiths to work at crude forges to hammer those woodsmen's tools into primitive but effective sabers.

The men of Williamsburg had further learned that Marion was a careful but skillful strategist. For hours he had questioned Major James, the captains of the Brigade's four companies, and anyone else who could give him information about the enemy's strength and situation, and then had laid his plans. He had decided that the port of Georgetown itself was far too well defended to offer a promising target, and had made up his mind to attack instead one of the Tory raiding parties operating in the neighborhood. The official functions of those parties were to recruit for the British army and forage for army supplies, but they usually made a habit of terrorizing the residents as well. To defeat even one such group would therefore serve several purposes. It would cool the ardor of Tory recruiting in the district; it would interfere with enemy supply deliveries; it would steady the morale of every Patriot who heard the news. The party Marion chose for his first adversary was the one led by a Major Gainey, whose sizable Tory force was stationed across the Pee Dee River, at a place called Britton's Neck between that river and the Little Pee Dee.

Over and over again Marion studied the maps his men drew for him in the sandy earth, until the route he would take and all its landmarks were perfectly clear in his mind. Then he issued orders that every man in the Brigade should fasten a small cockade of white paper in his cap, so that the Patriots could distinguish each other from the enemy even in the dark. At dusk he gave the order to march.

The column moved silently out of camp like a ghostly snake. Trails that were almost nonexistent quickly became invisible in the growing darkness. But Marion and his guides at the head of the line moved steadily forward. Sometimes swampy ground was sucking at the hoofs of their horses. Sometimes they were urging their mounts quietly up wooded slopes, or curbing the animals' tendency to break into a noisy gallop as they crossed a grass-scented meadow.

There was no pause for rest or food. Marion occasionally sipped at the vinegar-and-water he carried in his canteen, an acrid mixture that always made his friends wince but which remained his invariable drink in the field. A cold sweet potato served him for a meal as he rode on. And he paid his men the silent compliment of assuming that they could do with the same meager nourishment that satisfied his own tough, wiry body.

At dawn, from a sheltered vantage point, Marion was looking down on Gainey's encampment. Newly made fires were just beginning to spend spirals of smoke up into the still, gray air. Yawning men were moving slowly about among them, preparing their morning meal, stretching lazily, half awake. Off to one side Gainey's cavalrymen were feeding their horses. None of the Tories raised his head. It was clear that they had no suspicion of the Patriots staring down at them from a distance of only a few hundred yards.

Marion spoke under his breath to Major James and gestured toward the Tories' horses. The major collected a few companions and moved off. Marion waited until the little party had time to take up a position not far from the grassy area where the enemy's horses were tethered. Then he gave the rest of his men, still ranked behind him, the command to charge.

The loud thud of hoofs and a staccato rattle of shots broke the morning silence as the bulk of the Brigade swept headlong down upon their quarry, while James and his party rode swiftly in from the flank.

The Tories froze in their tracks. Every face was blank with complete and unbelieving surprise.

Dazedly, after a moment, some of them reached for their rifles. But already the Patriots were among them, slashing left and right with their home-made sabers, shouting at the tops of their lungs.

Suddenly the disorder became a rout. The Tories were running. Every man for himself, officers' half-spoken orders unheard or ignored, they were all making wildly for the shelter of the nearby swamp. Marion's men rode after them. But when they were certain that the fleeing enemy was too disorganized and panic-stricken to attempt a counterattack, they rode back again—with only two of their number even slightly wounded—to gather excitedly around the quiet little man who had planned and executed the morning's amazing affair.

The engagement had been over almost before it began. Assault had merged straight into victory.

It was a heady taste of triumph for the newly formed Brigade. The Patriots' spirits might have feasted on it for weeks. But while the grinning men with the white cockades in their hats were rewarding themselves with breakfast—borrowed, doubtless, from the abandoned Tory campfires—Marion was already planning their next move. He had scouts out on reconnaissance while the sun was still high. That afternoon, while most of his men were sleeping, he decided upon his next move. It was to be against a Captain Barfield, leader of a Tory band operating some miles further upstream along the Little Pee Dee. That same evening Marion ordered the Brigade on the march again for its second carefully planned raid.

Once more it was sunset as they mounted their horses and formed their columns. That was always Marion's favorite hour for starting a move through enemy country. But now the men rode with a new jauntiness and now their powder flasks were heavy with the precious gunpowder the Tories had left behind. They were better equipped for this attack and in high spirits—and that was fortunate indeed, because this time they did not find the Tories unprepared for their arrival.

Captain Barfield had his encampment well posted and his redcoats on the alert, probably as a result of having received news of Marion's disastrous attack on Gainey. He met Marion's dawn assault with such quick return fire that Marion instantly ordered a retreat.

But Marion didn't try to escape the Tories. In fact he made certain, as he and his men thudded away with every appearance of flight, that Barfield's troops were racing after them. And when Marion reached the spot where a little-known but shorter trail branched off from the one he was following, he sent part of his force off along it. The barely recognizable trace they would follow rejoined the main trail a little farther on, at a spot ideally suited for an ambush. Marion had given the detachment orders to wait in the thicket there until the Tories were led past that point by himself and the rest of his men, still playing hare to the Tory hounds along the main trail.

The Tories, rushing after him, were by then utterly contemptuous of their fleeing enemy. It never occurred to them to suspect trouble—until a volley of shots exploded in their very midst.

Horses reared, screaming. Men shouted furiously or in pain and reached frantically for their weapons. But they had no idea where to aim their fire. The Patriots hidden in the brush along the trail were completely invisible. Even while the Tories searched for targets, another volley showered death on their milling ranks.

Then, on the road in front of them, as if they had arisen out of the earth, Marion and the main body of his force reappeared. They had swung about and were now riding head on back into the crowd of soldiers choking the narrow road.

The Tories had no chance to attempt retaliation. They were too busy trying to turn their plunging mounts. Desperately they urged the foam-flecked animals into a bedlam-like retreat. Not all of them escaped, despite their desperate efforts.

Twice within twenty-four hours Marion and his Brigade had scattered an enemy force considerably stronger than themselves. But the unit was intact. Not a single Patriot had been killed.

Later that day, when the men had rested, Marion led them back to the Pee Dee, to a place along the river called Port's Ferry where he had decided to establish a camp. Their journey was a triumphal march. News of their two successes had already spread throughout the neighborhood, and all along the way Patriots rushed out of their doors to hail these new heroes and offer them food and drink.

Only the Tory-owned farm and plantation houses they passed remained bleakly shut, and it was easy to imagine the frightened families cowering inside them, or hiding in the nearby woods, convinced that their homes were about to be burned, their livestock stolen, their fields laid waste. None of those things happened. Marion had made it clear to his Brigade that he would stand for no useless destruction. A man who looted for personal gain was a criminal in his eyes; one who looted out of a spirit of vengeance—stealing or destroying Tory property because Tories had injured his own—was almost equally at fault. And so strong was Marion's influence over his men, even after their brief acquaintance with him, even though he had no legal hold over these volunteers, that most of them willingly accepted his standards as their own. Those who didn't, who saw no reason why they shouldn't benefit materially from their military victories, still controlled their greedy impulses out of a half-fearful respect for their little general's air of quiet authority.

At Port's Ferry, on the east bank of the Pee Dee, Marion had his men throw up a redoubt. He had managed to obtain two small and very old cannon, which he mounted on it, but because his supply of gunpowder was so small they were of little practical value. Nevertheless they gave an awesome look to the temporary fortifications, from which Marion could control the ferry crossing itself and Tory river traffic heading toward Georgetown with much-needed supplies for the British garrison there.

The whole neighborhood had taken on a new air of optimism within a few days. Patriots in the vicinity expected soon to hear that Gates had met and defeated Cornwallis' army. They had already heard that two other partisan bands, formed of volunteers like Marion's Brigade and led by Thomas Sumter and William Richardson Davie, were winning successes near the North Carolina border. The presence of Marion himself in their own area was fast dispelling dread of the enemy. Local Tory raiding parties, having learned of Gainey's and Barfield's fate, were disbanding entirely or moving closer to the protection of Georgetown. For the first time since the fall of Charleston the Patriots along the Pee Dee were beginning to look to the future with hope.

As for Marion, he was already planning to enlarge the scope of his activities, to repeat along the Santee River, closer to

Charleston, the tactics he had been using along the Pee Dee. For this purpose he himself prepared to march toward the upper Santee with most of his men, while he sent Peter Horry to cover the lower reaches of that river, to post guards at ferry crossings, to destroy any boats or canoes the enemy might otherwise make use of, and to gather all available information.

The letter of instructions Marion wrote to Horry on August 17, before the two separated, is firsthand evidence that in the five short days since his arrival in Williamsburg Marion had already adjusted himself to the difficulties of partisan fighting and established the pattern he would follow in the months to come.

The letter ordered Horry to take with him whatever men he could collect, presumably from local militia companies. Marion now bore the title of general, but he still could not forcibly draft men into his service. The letter also told Horry to collect, if possible, twenty-five pounds of gunpowder, along with a supply of balls or swanshot, and flints, and to send the ammunition to Kingstree so that Marion could pick it up there on his way to the upper Santee. Apparently this was the total amount of ammunition Marion expected to have on hand for his own expedition—and he was starting out lacking even that small supply. A postscript to the letter indicated that Horry would be no better off than his commander.

"You will . . . furnish your men with arms, wherever you can find them, giving receipts," Marion wrote.

Marion seemed to take for granted the fact that he lacked any official source of supplies, but he was beginning his partisan career as he meant to continue it: he would never take advantage of his authority as an officer to confiscate property for his Brigade's use without arranging for compensation to the owner. He had obtained President Rutledge's assurance that South Carolina would stand responsible for all materials of war her people furnished to the colony's defenders, and he intended to make certain that receipts were given for anything he and his men took—receipts that could someday be exchanged for government currency.

It was probably on the 18th of August that Marion and Horry both started out. Marion's own primary objective on this new expedition was a busy Santee crossing called Nelson's Ferry, on the main line of communication between Charleston and the important inland town of Camden. Cornwallis was known to have marched toward Camden, on his way to meet Gates' Patriot army, and Marion hoped to be able to destroy the British supply line from Charleston to that place.

But before Marion reached the Santee a courier from his Port's Ferry encampment overtook him with a grim message: Gates and Cornwallis had already met at Camden, and there the entire American army had been destroyed in a brief but furious battle. The few Patriots who had not been killed, seriously wounded or captured, had fled back toward North Carolina. Sumter's partisan force surprised by Tarleton's Rangers, had also been cut down. Nearly half Sumter's men had been taken prisoner; many had been killed. Sumter himself had barely escaped in the hideous confusion, first by hiding under a wagon and then by riding alone and at night to Davie's headquarters at Charlotte, North Carolina, where he arrived on a saddleless horse and without a coat to his back. Gates was at the same place, having galloped seventy miles in a desperate dash for safety after witnessing the tragic collapse of all his grandiose hopes.

The news would have overwhelmed most men in Marion's position. It meant not only the end of his confident belief that the Patriots were about to retake South Carolina. It meant that he himself was the only Patriot commander still at large in the state, that he had been left as the single target upon whom all enemy efforts would now be concentrated.

Marion received the dispatch so calmly, however, that his men didn't even suspect its contents. He didn't tell them the bad news. He had decided that the dangers that faced him would not become really serious for another day or two. For that long, he thought, the British would be too busy to look for trouble. They would be taking care of their own wounded from the Battle of Camden, preparing them for the journey to Charleston. They would also be making up convoys of American prisoners to be sent to that same place. And they would almost certainly remain in their present camp, near Camden, until they received new supplies from the coast. All these activities would mean heavy traffic along the Santee, and this might have seemed a good reason for Marion to leave that neighborhood. But he had made up his mind instead to seize the opportunity that traffic offered, and to attempt at least one lightning raid. He would have to work fast, before the British were alerted to his presence. But he thought they didn't yet suspect his nearness, and was convinced they wouldn't anticipate an American attack on the very heels of such a disastrous American defeat.

Coolly, therefore, as if that dispatch had contained no news worthy of comment, Marion continued to lead his Brigade toward Nelson's Ferry.

The night of August 20 found the partisans moving quietly along treacherous swamp paths close to the river. When he was still some distance from Nelson's Ferry, Marion halted to give his men a brief rest while scouts went forward to study the condition of the river crossing itself and the roads leading to it. But the scouts returned before they had gone that far. Only a short distance from the place where the Brigade lay hidden in the swamp, they reported a convoy of American prisoners, on its way to Charleston, encamped for the night. The prisoners were guarded by soldiers, and there were pickets surrounding the sleeping men and a group of supply wagons. Most of the accompanying British, including all the officers, were inside a house close by, having left their arms stacked at the door under guard.

Marion decided to attack immediately. By the light of a flaring pine knot he studied the sketch his scouts drew in the sand, and made his plans.

He himself, with most of his men, would make the primary

assault on the British position by approaching the British-occupied house from the rear. In the meantime Colonel Hugh Horry, Peter's brother, would take sixteen men by a circle route through the swamp to a position on the road leading away from the house. Marion's idea was that if the British managed to collect their prisoners and lead them quickly away from his assaulting party, Horry would be able to halt them there long enough for Marion to come up and attack a second time.

Just before dawn Horry and his men vanished through the trees to take up their places, and Marion led his party in the other direction. Rifles and pistols were freshly primed, and the Patriots rode with their hands on their sabers.

But while Marion was still some distance from the house a shot rang out, followed immediately by loud yells and the pounding feet of horses. Horry's party had come upon a sentry outpost quick-witted enough to fire the moment he saw the intruders. Horry, realizing that the shot would alert the enemy, was riding full tilt for the house. He and his men were making as much noise as possible. Their only hope now lay in convincing the British that they were about to be attacked by a sizable force.

Swiftly but silently Marion and his men drew closer to the building to support the attack that was now inevitable. Horry had already reached it before they arrived. He and his small party swooped down on the stacked arms and overcame the soldiers in charge of them. Then, leaving a few of their number outside to mount guard over the guns, Horry and the rest burst into the house and demanded its instantaneous surrender. The redcoated officers, forced to submit, listened hopefully for sounds of rescue from the guards outside.

But those guards were now facing a new enemy. Marion and his party had come up, slipping shadow-like from tree to tree and running bent over through the tall grass. British soldiers were very seldom excellent shots, and this time they seemed to be aiming at ghosts. They kept up a steady firing, but one by one they were picked off by their unseen assailants. Within a few minutes all British resistance had ceased entirely, and Marion's Brigade herded the last of the British and Tory soldiers into a subdued group near the house.

Then Marion released the American prisoners, all Continentals from Maryland, whom the British had been convoying to the prison ships in Charleston harbor.

The gaunt, hungry Marylanders, who had fallen asleep the night before assuming that they were on their way to those odorous floating jails, were almost tearfully grateful to their rescuers. But they immediately dampened the spirits of Marion's men, elated until then over one more victory under Marion's leadership, by telling them of Gates' defeat. The men heard the news in stunned silence, unaware that their general had known it for some hours and had managed to show them only his usual calm determination.

The members of the Brigade couldn't take the news so calmly, especially when the former prisoners told them in detail about the shockingly poor generalship that had brought about the loss of almost the entire American force at Camden. Even if it was true that Gates himself had escaped, the prisoners pointed out, the future of the Patriot cause in the South looked poor indeed if Gates was to remain its champion. Some of them said grimly that they would return home and join some other Maryland outfit, to continue the fight in the north. Marion offered the rest membership in his Brigade. Only three accepted. Those who refused declared that in their opinion the war—in the South, at least—was already over, and that they saw no point in risking their lives trying to revive a lost cause.

This too, of course, further depressed Marion's men, who realized now that they were the only Patriot force still at large in all of South Carolina. Some of them, during the march back to the Port's Ferry camp, slipped away from the lines and returned to their own homes. They left for various reasons. Those who had originally joined the Brigade only with the hope of sharing in any loot it might seize—there were always a few such men in any army—had already learned that opportunities for looting were rare under Marion's watchful eyes; now those particular men were glad of an excuse to give up a profitless venture. Others told Marion, truthfully, that they were worried about the safety of their families now that British control of the state was again complete, and felt they should go back home to protect their wives and children from enemy raiding parties. In still other cases the men were leaving—sometimes quietly at night, without a word of good-by—because they had become convinced that the cause Marion represented was utterly hopeless and not worth further sacrifice.

Marion let them all go, without protest. In the first place he had no power to hold any man against his will. But Marion would not have forced them to stay if he could. He didn't want to fight with unwilling warriors. And he hoped that if he offered no objection to these sudden departures, at least some of the men would return when he could again offer them a real chance to strike at the enemy.

By the time he reached his base at Port's Ferry there were only one hundred and fifty men still with him. Together with Peter Horry's little force, on the lower Santee, they stood alone in South Carolina against Cornwallis and his entire army and his Tory allies. And Cornwallis was now ready to focus his attention on Marion's Brigade.

The British general had regarded the rout of Gainey's force humiliating but unimportant; any commander might occasionally be taken by surprise and driven into retreat. The defeat of Barfield the next day, since Barfield had been ready for the Patriots, had been harder to accept. Marion's recapture of the one hundred and fifty American prisoners Cornwallis saw as an unforgivable blow to British prestige. Determined to destroy this ragged partisan once and for all, he sent a Major James Wemyss into the district between the Santee and the Pee Dee to carry out the task.

Wemyss took with him his own 63rd Regiment and a strong body of Tories led by a Major Harrison, who knew the district well—and was known there as one of the most hated and feared of Tory despoilers and looters. Even Harrison's unsavory reputation, however, soon paled alongside that of Wemyss, who came to be regarded as one of the most ruthless officers in the British ranks.

Swift-riding couriers brought Marion the news of Wemyss' approach. Marion immediately called in Peter Horry's raiding party and dispatched Major James with a small body of picked men to scout the oncoming British. His orders to James were strict. The little scouting party was on no account to engage the enemy; its only function was to observe and report Wemyss' strength. James nodded his understanding and departed. Marion himself then ordered the remnants of his Brigade into marching order and moved slowly off in the same general direction James had taken, in order to be as near Wemyss as possible in case James recommended an immediate attack.

From trusted friends James was soon able to pinpoint exactly the British line of march, and to learn that it was following the rough road through Kingstree. James hurried to that place, chose cover alongside the road, and ordered his men to dismount and take posts from which they could watch the trail through the tangled underbrush. Night had fallen and a bright moon had climbed high in the sky when one of James' scouts crept close to him to report that the vanguard of the enemy was approaching.

Almost immediately the Patriots' horses picked up the scent of the still-invisible marchers. Every man in James's party clamped one hand on his horse's bridle and kept the other ready to stifle a betraying whinny.

Finally came the quiet thud of horses' hoofs in the distance. A few moments later the first mounted redcoats swung into view. They were well-trained men. Their hands were on their pistols, their heads turned from left to right and back again as they inspected the green walls between which they were traveling. James could see the buttons glint on their uniforms as they rode past, but he and his men were well protected in their hiding place. The enemy vanguard rode on out of sight.

After only a few moments of silence the Patriots heard new sounds—this time the dull, scuffling noises made by men marching along a sandy, rutted trail. Tensely they watched the stretch of road within their range of vision, and caught their breath at what appeared. Rank upon rank of soldiers were moving past them. The knapsack on every shoulder looked well filled, and the powder flask and cartridge pouch swinging from each broad belt was obviously heavy. It was easy to count them. They numbered three hundred—twice the size of Marion's force. It was easy to see, too, that Wemyss was an excellent soldier despite his unenviable reputation for brutality. He was using Marion's tactics, marching by night and in stealth.

When the body of British regulars had disappeared the men with James glanced uneasily at each other and then away again. The force they had just seen represented a formidable enemy.

There was no opportunity to share more than troubled looks. Almost on the heels of the disappearing marchers came more men, some mounted, some on foot. Their uniforms indicated that they were Tories, but they too were well equipped. They numbered five hundred.

When the last of them had finally passed, James' men moved to gather about him, ready to ride northward at top speed to report to Marion the approaching enemy's strength. They had scarcely exchanged a whispered word or two when once more sounds drifted to their ears from up the road. Once more, peering from their safe cover, they watched a body of Tories approach, again partly on foot and partly mounted.

Major James studied this group intently. It was not like the ones that had gone before. It might be a rear guard that had grown overconfident and forgotten to be vigilant. It might be simply a party of stragglers incompetent to keep up with the main body of Wemyss' men. In any case it moved lazily, in disordered lines. It lacked discipline and any evidence of alertness.

Suddenly, silently, Major James swung up into his saddle and gestured commandingly to his men. He remembered Marion's orders, but the Tories now nearing the Patriot hiding place offered too powerful a temptation for a partisan to resist. His tight-lipped followers, stealthily mounting their own horses, were just as eager to strike as he was.

An instant later, when the Tories came directly opposite the thicket where he hid, the partisans burst out upon them. Rifle shots cracked like thunder and sabers glinted wickedly in the moonlight. Pandemonium broke loose among the Tories.

James and his men snatched at the reins of riderless mounts, fired a few final shots, and then with James in the lead tore off down the road over which the Tories had just come. Already in the distance they could hear Wemyss' main force charging back to investigate the resounding shots that had stopped them in their tracks. But James was leaving no trace of his slashing attack except the dead and wounded Tories that lay sprawled in the sandy ruts of the moonlit trail. Wemyss made no attempt to track down the mysterious assailants. Before dawn James had rejoined Marion.

General Marion listened quietly to a breathless account of the strength of Wemyss' army. To some of the officers, gathered with him around the returned scouting party, the wealth of equipment Wemyss carried with him offered an exciting challenge. Eagerly they waited for their commander to map out the attack that would win some of that valuable ammunition for their own ill-equipped band. To others the most important aspect of James' story was the tragic future it foretold for the whole district, unless Wemyss could be frightened away from the area; those men too looked hopefully to Marion to give them their orders for a brilliant surprise assault that would cripple the British leader's army.

Marion dashed all their hopes with the first word he spoke. Skillfully as he could use the weapon of surprise, he fully recognized its limits. If he attacked Wemyss now he believed there could be only one result of the engagement: his Brigade would be utterly overwhelmed, perhaps even completely annihilated. Therefore he would not attack. In order to preserve a nucleus of the Brigade, safe and ready for future action, Marion proposed to lead his men away from Wemyss rather than toward him. He announced that the Brigade would return immediately to Port's Ferry, remain there only long enough to break up its encampment, and then continue northward by forced marches until it had passed beyond the boundary of the state.

The courage of Marion's decision was not apparent to all his men. Those who could recognize courage only in action muttered that they would leave his service rather than join in such a disgraceful retreat. Others, aware that Marion was taking the only possible course in a perilous moment, nevertheless declared that they too would stay behind because they dared not leave their families unprotected with Wemyss in the neighborhood.

Marion understood both points of view. He didn't attempt to argue with either. His own duty, as he saw it, was simply to lead the Brigade and determine its course of action. It was the responsibility of each Brigade member to remain with the unit, or to leave it, as he saw fit.

On August 28, when Marion abandoned the Port's Ferry camp and headed northward, the majority of his officers went with him, but no more than sixty of his men. They traveled night and day, stopping only when the horses could go no further without rest. On the way they discarded their two small cannon because Marion had reached the conclusion that heavy artillery was too much of a burden to partisans. They didn't halt until they were at the headwaters of the Waccamaw, in the southeastern corner of North Carolina not many miles inland from the coast.

Major James and his scouts had gone with Marion only part of the way and they had spent the journey discussing future plans. Then James returned southward again, to maintain a secret watch on the British and keep Marion informed about the possibility of raising new recruits for the Brigade. Wemyss could be attacked only if the Brigade were considerably larger than it had been in the past. If a sizable force were waiting to join him, Marion himself would return to the district between the Pee Dee and the Santee, because the moment would then have arrived to re-enter the fight. But both James and Marion knew that the British general's presence in the area might terrify most of the neutrals into overtly joining the British, and might even convince ardent Patriots that further resistance to England was utterly useless.

What the future held for Marion he could not guess as he said a quiet good-by to Major James and rode on northward without him. He was acutely aware that he was leaving his state unprotected by any organized band of troops; in the eyes of some men he might thus be laying himself open to a suspicion of cowardice and desertion. But preserving the core of his Brigade seemed to Marion his chief duty at the moment, and if others saw his behavior in a different light he would not spend his energies in an effort to correct them. All his energies were still concentrated on the cause that remained the motivating force in his life, even though that cause now looked so hopeless to many who had been his brothers-in-arms only a short time before.

CHAPTER X

Life in the little camp of exile along the Waccamaw was not easy. There were enough Tories in the neighborhood to be a constant source of danger, even though Marion knew they were not sufficiently well organized to threaten him with an outright assault. But to guard against hit-and-run sorties he had to post his exhausted men on twenty-four-hour picket duty. To protect his foraging parties—the Brigade still had to find food for itself and its horses—he had to restrict their activities to a small area. The supplies that could be obtained under such circumstances were meager and monotonous.

Sweet potatoes roasted in a fire were the staple—sometimes the only—food in camp. Ears of roasted corn, or hulled kernels of corn boiled to make hominy, occasionally took their place. Rice was usually unobtainable; the rice-growing areas near the coast were in British hands. Meat was a rarity and never very good. Farmers had learned during the long years of the war to hide their animals deep in the forest, where constant roaming for food developed more sinew than fat and flavor.

Two things might have made this dull and inadequate diet a little more palatable. One was salt, the other was rum. Marion's Brigade had neither. Salt was almost never seen anywhere in the country by then, except right along the coast where enterprising men produced a coarse variety by evaporating sea water. Ten silver dollars a bushel was the price being asked for it by 1780, and that price translated into Continental paper currency would probably have filled a bushel basket in itself. But the price of salt was an academic question so far as Marion and his men were concerned; they had no money of any kind.

As for rum, Marion's men were not part of the Continental Army that still sometimes received official rations of this usual soldier's drink. Continental soldiers had been known to desert during periods when rum was not issued, but Marion's men were learning to be grateful when the water they drank came from a clear stream rather than from a stagnant swamp. Perhaps the vinegar Marion added to his own canteen became a habit simply because it masked the taste and smell of the brownish swamp water that all too often washed down his dinner of unsalted, unaccompanied potatoes.

But the monotony of the meals in the Waccamaw camp, and the strain of always being on guard, were minor irritations compared to the mounting tension Marion's men felt about conditions in their home district.

By the end of the first week in exile Marion had received word from Major James that Wemyss was systematically looting a strip of Williamsburg country seventy miles long and fifteen miles wide. What livestock, stored grain and other property he couldn't carry off he destroyed. Local Tories were also doing a lively looting business of their own. When Wemyss rode into a new settlement they hurried to give him the names of its Patriots or suspected Patriots, in return for which Weymss permitted them to take what they wanted from each victim's house before it was burned to the ground. Sometimes the Tories offered Wemyss the name of a man whose sympathies had always been neutral, or even pro-British, simply because his horses or silver had aroused their greed.

James' reports made grim reading. Wemyss seemed very quickly to be achieving his purpose of punishing the inhabitants of Williamsburg for having defied English authority, and of bringing the district to its knees. Many neutrals, wanting only the restoration of order—and however outraged some of them might be over the losses they had suffered—were making up their minds that only England was powerful enough to restore the area to order once more. Even many Patriots were deciding that further resistance to England's strength was both foolish and impossible. Some were even turning Tory themselves in the hope of regaining, as loot, what they had already lost during Tory-inspired raids.

To Marion and his followers it seemed all too likely that every man in Williamsburg would soon be frightened or lured into submission and lost forever to the Patriot cause. Every day the possibility of winning new recruits for Marion's Brigade appeared to grow less and less.

Studying the gaunt, drawn faces of the men around his campfires, Marion wondered how long they would remain with him. Each message from James made them more concerned over the fate of their families and friends back home. They were growing desperate for revenge. The time might come very soon when they would leave the Waccamaw one by one—if Marion did not lead them forth as a group—to attempt some secret and personal retaliation of their own.

Marion was as eager to return to South Carolina as they were, although revenge formed no part of his motive. But he too was worried about the Williamsburg people, and equally worried about a great many others as well. He knew that once Williamsburg was thoroughly defeated, every area in the colony that had shown any resistance to England would receive the same treatment. Afterward Cornwallis and his officers would carry the war beyond South Carolina's boundary. North Carolina would be their next target, Virginia the one after that. All America might soon be in British hands. Cornwallis was already so confident that he was gathering supplies at Camden for the first leg of his journey north.

Marion knew all this, and knew he was helpless to combat it. The number of men with him—scarcely more than half a hundren—was not enough for a swift raid on Cornwallis' supply lines. It was certainly not enough of a force to lead out against

Wemyss' swollen strength. Marion was doing the only thing he could do: trying to remain calm enough to keep his men calm and under control.

It was Wemyss himself who finally released Marion from his difficult role, and sooner than Marion had dared to hope. He did it by overplaying his hand. Instead of halting his march of destruction when it had begun to achieve the results he wanted, and turning his attention to a program that would offer the neutrals some promise of the order they longed for and the Patriots some hope of a generous peace, Wemyss continued to pile devastation upon devastation.

No field was too large, no kitchen garden patch too small, for his men to raid. The handsomest plantation house and the most modest cabin were looted and set afire with equal enthusiasm. Major James' own home was burned to the ground and his entire plantation despoiled with painstaking thoroughness. Every one of his books was heaped upon the flames and every scrap of paper found in the house was added to the conflagration.

By these and similar depredations—by showing the same lack of perception that marked so many similar British actions during the Revolution—Wemyss was beginning to lose the allies he had originally won. His own callous brutality and the license he allowed his followers were transforming neutrality into alarm and fright into hatred. Men who had made up their minds to submit to the British out of terror or self-interest were changing their opinion. Their only chance of survival, many of them came to feel, lay not in joining Wemyss but in ridding themselves of his presence. They began to slip away to hide in the woods and the swamps, and to send word to Major James that they wished Marion would return to the district to lead them out against the enemy.

When the news reached Waccamaw, at the end of Marion's second week there, he and his men filled their canteens, stuffed sweet potatoes and ears of corn into their pouches, slung their saddles over their horses' backs, and took off immediately.

In less than a single day they had once more reached the

South Carolina border. Marion had led them along the Little Pee Dee, across that river and the Big Pee Dee, and on to the Lynches River. There, in territory familiar to Marion, at a rendezvous arranged through Major James, they met a force of some hundred men captained by Henry Mouzon and Major James' cousin, also named John James.

There, too, they heard the bitterly disappointing news that Weymss was now beyond their reach. Leaving a Captain John Coming Ball and a sizable force of Tories in Williamsburg to continue his work there, Weymss had returned with most of his redcoats to Georgetown on the coast. And Georgetown's defenses were far too strong to be assaulted by a scant hundred and fifty partisans.

"Then we'll fight Ball!" the men said.

Marion was not certain that even this was wise until additional recruits had joined his group, but he knew his men too well to argue. He could control their impatient tempers no longer. A moment later he was watching Mouzon and James scratch maps on the ground and plan how best to surprise a foe who would have the advantage over his own Brigade in manpower and position.

Ball was encamped just then at a place called Shepard's Ferry, on the far side of the Black Mingo Creek. The Black Mingo, too deep to ford in that immediate neighborhood, could be crossed in only two ways: by the ferry itself or by the bridge a mile farther upstream.

The ferry would be closely guarded. Marion immediately discarded the idea of using it, although it would have given him direct passage to the house Ball was using as his headquarters— a house standing on the road leading away from the ferry toward the south. The bridge might be guarded too. Men passing over it in narrow file might be picked off before reaching the farther side. They might even be picked off before that, because they would have to approach the bridge by a long causeway through a swamp, and that causeway might also be guarded. But the bridge was the only possibility that presented itself. If they negotiated it safely, Marion explained to his officers, they would then follow the trail on the far side that led downstream to Shepard's Ferry and Ball's headquarters there.

Once the plan was clearly understood, Marion gave his eager men the order to mount. By midnight his quietly moving ranks of horsemen had reached the boggy causeway that stretched between them and the bridge. Scouts sent ahead returned to whisper triumphantly that the causeway and the bridge itself were both unguarded. The partisans swift return from North Carolina was evidently unsuspected by the Tories. Marion nodded, touched his horse's flank, and led his men forward.

As he himself rode over the bridge he was acutely aware that the hoofs of the partisans' horses were thudding hollowly against the wooden planking. At every step waves of sound reverberated through the quiet night. Never again, Marion resolved, would he cross a bridge without first covering its planks with all the blankets the Brigade carried. But it was too late to repair the damage now.

Scarcely half his men had followed him off the far end of the bridge when he heard the alarm gun he had been expecting. Its loud boom echoing across the fields from Shepard's Ferry, still a mile away downstream, told him that he had already lost his one advantage—surprise.

Instantly Marion plunged forward into the darkness. At a mad pace his men rode after him downstream until they were within three hundred yards of the house where Ball and his officers were bivouacked. There they pulled up to an abrupt halt and dismounted.

There were no lights in the house up ahead, and no sound anywhere. The silence was ominous. Marion knew that the Tories were by now prepared for an attack, but he could not guess where they had stationed themselves. The numerous advantages the enemy had originally possessed were now trebled.

Quietly he divided his men into four small groups and sent three of them forward on foot immediately—one by the road that led directly toward the house, the other two by the open fields to the left and right of the road. Marion himself would wait until the Tories were already engaged and then bring up the fourth group, mounted, as a reserve force.

Colonel Hugh Horry was in charge of the group that moved out into the fields to the right. His little party was still some distance away from the building, visible only as a threatening dark mass against the sky, when the night was shattered by explosions of sound and bursts of light. Several men in Horry's front ranks dropped. The rest fell back, staggered by the suddenness of the attack and the fact that it had come from some undetermined place directly in front of them—from the fields that still stretched ahead in what was now utter darkness again. Then another Tory volley rang out and another. The cries of Horry's wounded were telling the enemy where the Patriots were, but the Tories' momentary musket flashes were not providing the confused Americans with targets.

Captain James, with Horry's men, shouted at them to fall prone, to fire from the ground, but not to retreat. Horry was shouting too, assuring the men that the enemy was dead ahead, that they could not fail to strike a Tory if they aimed straight forward.

Slowly, one by one, the partisans' guns began to answer the Tory muzzle flashes. But more cries of wounded men mingled with the crackle of musket fire, and the meager strength of the little group was being reduced by each fusillade from the invisible guns that had so successfully found the range.

Then, suddenly, shots rang out from far up ahead, from beyond the place where the Tories were hidden. With a great surge of relief Horry and James realized that one of the other partisan groups had come up on the Tories' flank.

From that moment the tide turned. The Tories, caught in a vicious crossfire, began to edge out of the hiding place that had become a trap. Their fire slackened as they crept toward the safety of Black Mingo Creek. When Marion raced up with his reserves, almost immediately afterward, the cautious Tory retreat turned into a dash for safety. Within a matter of minutes, abandoning their wounded in the bloody field, they were escaping into the depths of the Black Mingo Swamp.

The Brigade had turned a defeat into a victory. Marion's men counted sixty Tory dead and wounded on the battlefield. Among their victims was Captain Ball himself, and the partisans turned over his splendid mount to their Brigade commander. Marion named the animal Ball, in honorable tribute to the enemy who had so nearly defeated him, and the big, handsome horse carried him through many battles from then on.

The triumph had cost the Brigade a heavy price. One third of Marion's men were killed or wounded. The battle did, however, achieve a purpose. It restored the courage and hope of the Patriots of Williamsburg. It shattered the British complacency over Wemyss' success there, and had a powerful effect on the local Tories. Some withdrew to the protection of their English friends at Georgetown. Some went into hiding. Still others, who had not always called themselves Tories in the past, presented themselves to Marion and asked to join his Brigade.

Marion didn't refuse these new recruits, even though some of them had changed their colors more than once within the past few weeks—had actually in certain cases served under Marion originally, deserted to the British, and were now turncoats a third time. Marion's officers were suspicious, but Marion understood that what appeared to be vacillation or treachery might instead be ignorance or misunderstanding of the complexities of the Revolution itself. Many men had been honestly confused between loyalty to the King and loyalty to a new rebel government —a practically nonexistent government. It made them, in a sense, innocent bystanders, caught between two forces that pushed them first one way and then the other, depending on which was stronger at any particular moment. So when Marion welcomed these new recruits into his Brigade it was not only because he needed men; it was also with the hope that he could help them come to understand and share his own unswerving devotion to independence from England.

Even with these new recruits, however, the Brigade shrank

noticeably again after the defeat of the Tories at Shepard's Ferry. Most of the men who had rendezvoused with Marion on his return from the Waccamaw asked him immediately after the battle for permission to return to their families. They said they wanted to rebuild their burned homes before winter set in —it was then the middle of September—and to harvest whatever crops had escaped the raiders' fires. Marion agreed that they had to look after their families. But he realized that some of the men considered the Revolution already won as far as Williamsburg was concerned, and that the Williamsburg Revolution was the only one they cared about. And to these men Marion tried to explain how much the Patriots still had to accomplish before they could expect to live in real peace and security. He let them go, of course, but he did ask them to rejoin him as soon as they put their personal affairs in order. The place he chose for a rendezvous on that occasion was little Snow Island, between the Lynches and the Pee Dee rivers, where those two streams joined.

Marion and the small party remaining with him then spent the next few days relaxing not far from that island, among friendly planters whose lands had not yet been burned or despoiled by the enemy. There they were warmly greeted and well fed, and Ball and the rest of the mounts could wander freely through rich pastures. The Patriots were badly in need of this relaxation, but Marion felt he had no right to rest. Soon he was sending regular couriers to Snow Island to find out whether the absent members of his Brigade were reassembling there. The moment he had a force to command again he wanted to be back in the fight.

A week went by, and another week. Still not a single Brigade member had appeared at the island. Marion was beginning to despair. He decided that the men of Williamsburg had found his plea unconvincing, that they were no longer willing to fight for freedom now that their own district seemed free of the enemy.

If that was the case, Marion felt, if he had no Brigade to command, then he must put himself and the few men with him under the command of some other Patriot officer. He suggested to his little party of faithful followers that they ride north again across the border to Hillsboro, where they could join Gates, who was trying to collect the demoralized remnants of his broken army, or the partisan companies led by Davie or Sumter.

There was plenty of work for Patriots to do in North Carolina, Marion knew. He had learned that Cornwallis had already begun his march northward and had reached the town of Charlotte, North Carolina. And though Marion realized the Patriots might not be strong enough to stop the British advance at that point, he felt they could at least be raiding the long enemy supply lines, now stretching all the way from Charlotte back to Charleston.

Hugh Horry argued vehemently against this plan. He was convinced that Marion would be more effective as an independent commander than as part of a large and more regimented army. Horry was also convinced that Marion's men would eventually return. They had probably found far greater difficulties awaiting them at home than they had expected, he pointed out, but he was certain that most of them meant to rejoin the Brigade as soon as they were able.

Marion listened and agreed to wait another few days. At the end of that time the men did begin to appear at Snow Island—one by one, in two's and three's, in groups of half a dozen at a time. Marion wasted no time berating them for their tardiness. Instead he started off immediately for the camp along Lynches River where the Tories now had their headquarters, commanded by one of the two Harrison brothers who had long been among the most active and hated British adherents in that part of Carolina.

But before the newly reorganized Brigade could reach the Harrison camp, Marion learned about another concentration farther south along the Black River. There, at a place called Tarcote, a Colonel Tynes was busily—and successfully, Marion's scouts reported—recruiting local Tories under the British flag. The scouts also assured Marion that Tynes had a very large supply of equipment—muskets, bayonets, swords, pistols, powder and bullets, even saddles and bridles—which he was lavishly distributing to those who joined him. Marion instantly swung around toward the south and headed for Tarcote at top speed. He had made up his mind that that equipment would be very useful to his own Brigade.

As usual, Marion's timing was good. It was just before midnight when he halted his men at a point several miles from the Tynes camp and ordered them to snatch what rest they could while a handful of scouts moved silently forward through the woods to spy out the enemy's situation. The scouts returned in high good humor. Tynes, they told Marion, had posted no sentinels at all. His campfires were burning brightly against the autumn chill, and his men were grouped snugly around them, some fast asleep and the rest engrossed in games of cards.

Marion roused his men and led them forward through the woods until they could peer through trees and underbrush at the relaxed and unsuspecting Tories. An instant later he gave the order for attack, and the Patriots rushed into the circle of campfires, shouting and firing noisily.

For a brief moment the Tories simply stared, as if they thought they must be dreaming. Cards slipped from fingers suddenly limp. Men roused from sleep lay unmoving on the ground, blinking in utter amazement. Then the Tories leaped to their feet and ran. Jostling frantically against each other, some still trailing blankets behind them, they disappeared into the nearby Tarcote Swamp.

They vanished so fast that the Brigade killed only two of them and caught only Tynes himself and some twenty of his followers before they escaped. The Tories had not even slightly wounded a single one of Marion's men.

Afterward, while the grinning Patriots enjoyed the warmth of the enemy's campfires and helped themselves to the plentiful food and drink the enemy had left behind, Marion inventoried the supplies that had fallen so painlessly into his hands. For the first time in his partisan career he could adequately arm his whole Brigade, distribute to each man as much ammunition as he could carry, and still hold in reserve a sizable amount of matériel. It was probably this unaccustomed wealth that made Marion decide, on the spot, to return to Snow Island and establish there some sort of permanent camp—a place where he could store his recently acquired supplies and any others he might seize in the future, a place where his men could rest between forays, where recruits could gather and where prisoners could be held until it was safe or convenient to forward them to some more central point or exchange them for captured Patriots.

Snow Island proved as ideal for Marion's purpose as he had sensed it would be. The water that surrounded it was in turn surrounded by almost impenetrable swamps and woods. Within a few weeks, while some of Marion's men kept up a series of raids on various small Tory concentrations in the area, the rest of the Brigade transformed it into an unwalled but remarkably safe fortress.

All the streams for miles around were scoured for boats, and those not needed for transportation back and forth to the moss-hung citadel were carefully destroyed. All the bridges in the vicinity were burned. Trees were felled across all trails approaching the neighborhood. From concealed guardposts established in concentric rings around the island, sentinels could communicate with each other and with the camp itself by calls indistinguishable from bird cries. Even Marion's own foraging and raiding parties, returning to headquarters, had to identify themselves beyond question before boats were rowed across the water to take them back to Snow Island. It seemed unlikely that a stranger could ever penetrate even to the outermost ring of Marion's pickets, but if any should do so the Brigade would certainly be alerted to his presence long before he could come close to the island itself.

The establishment of a permanent base marked a turn in the tide of the Brigade's affairs. And by late October, when work on Snow Island was about completed, the whole course of the

Revolution seemed to take a new turn. Word reached Marion then of the amazing Patriot success at King's Mountain.

There, on a craggy hilltop, just north of the South Carolina border, a thousand Tories commanded by Major Patrick Ferguson had all been killed, wounded or taken prisoner by a hastily assembled force of rifle-shooting farmers and hunters from Tennessee, Virginia and North Carolina. Ferguson had been raiding and recruiting west of Charlotte, where Cornwallis was encamped, and serving as Cornwallis' left flank during the British general's move northward. The defeat of Ferguson's entire force—Ferguson himself had been killed at King's Mountain—so thoroughly alarmed Cornwallis that he abandoned his campaign and retreated desperately southward, hurrying his men back through autumn rain and mud until they reached Winnsboro, South Carolina.

But even in South Carolina, Cornwallis found no rest, although he had left that state under the presumably iron control of Wemyss and other British officers. Now the situation was considerably changed. Now the partisan bands of Sumter and Davie were fearlessly raiding the area around his own camp at Winnsboro. Now the British supply lines from Charleston to Winnsboro were regularly disrupted by Marion's men. And Marion was making other kinds of trouble too. His Brigade had grown so daring that, as Cornwallis frantically reported, it "carried terror to the gates of Charleston." It had also grown so large, since the Battle of King's Mountain, that it drew from Cornwallis another despairing admission. In a letter to Sir Henry Clinton—who less than six months before had declared there were "few men in South Carolina who are not either our prisoners or in arms with us"—Cornwallis had to confess that by late in the year 1780 there was "scarce an inhabitant" between the Santee and the Pee Dee who was not in arms *against* the British. Since Marion's arrival in Williamsburg that district had been transformed into an open mockery of England's claim to the possession of all South Carolina.

Cornwallis decided that at all costs Marion's Brigade must be destroyed. He assigned that task to that hard-riding, hard-fighting Legion commander, Colonel Banastre Tarleton.

Tarleton accepted the assignment enthusiastically. He was contemptuous of all rebels and particularly of the ragged partisans. Taking a small troop of cavalry with him from Winnsboro and planning to rendezvous along the road with his own veteran Legion—then stationed thirty miles to the east at Camden—he set off toward the coast and the easy victory he anticipated.

Marion received word, through Patriot friends, that Tarleton was on his way. But the details of the intelligence that reached him were mistaken and helped set in motion a comedy of errors played out between Marion and the most dangerous enemy he had yet encountered. It was a comedy that might well have had a tragic ending for the little Brigade commander.

Believing that Tarleton's Legion would not join its commander before Tarleton reached Nelson's Ferry on the Santee, and sure that his own swift Brigade could reach that point in time to ambush the small troop of cavalry escorting Tarleton, Marion set out at top speed. At Nelson's Ferry he learned that the British had passed that place two days earlier, still traveling eastward and apparently with no idea that Marion was behind them. Marion did not learn, however, that the main body of the Legion had already joined the small troop of cavalry. So Marion took off in pursuit of a much superior force, confident that he could defeat Tarleton as soon as he caught up with him.

By nightfall the Brigade had covered a considerable distance. Marion assumed that Tarleton still had the best part of a two-day lead, however, and was impatient to press on, but necessity forced him to allow his saddle-weary men a brief rest. They were dismounted and relaxing in the shelter of a thick wood when the sky just ahead began to glow with the unmistakable light of flames.

Instantly Marion changed his plans. That glow indicated to him that almost certainly, somewhere not far off, a large dwelling or large barn was burning. The only such buildings in the neighborhood, he knew, were on the plantation of a Colonel

Richardson. Richardson himself, an ardent Patriot, had fallen into British hands at the defeat of Charleston. Marion felt sure that the destruction of a Patriot's unprotected home was the sort of temptation Tarleton could not resist, even if it meant a delay in his original schedule.

Convinced therefore, that his enemy was close at hand, and that the cavalrymen with him would be too busy plundering to be alert to trouble, Marion ordered his own followers to remount in preparation for a surprise assault.

Marion was giving instructions to his officers when a dozen Patriot muskets suddenly swung into position, aimed at a shadowy figure just emerging from the trees. One of the officers uttered a name in amazement. The figure was that of Colonel Richardson. Marion stepped quickly forward with words of congratulation for the colonel's escape from Charleston and of sympathy for Tarleton's presence on his place. But Richardson had come for neither. He had had reason to believe Marion was there in the woods—had been searching for him with a desperate purpose.

Richardson told his grim story in a few words. Tarleton had descended upon his plantation earlier that day, and so swiftly that the Patriot had barely been able to flee into hiding in the forest. From there he had watched Tarleton's men strip his house from top to bottom, and then had heard Tarleton give the order to set it afire. It was shortly before the blaze was lit that a stranger approached Tarleton. Richardson had not recognized him, but from his dress he felt sure he had been a partisan and was probably a deserter from Marion's Brigade. And Richardson had seen enough of what went on to realize that Tarleton was being told of Marion's close presence in the neighborhood and being warned of a probable partisan attack. Richardson concluded his account with a description of Tarleton's force.

For the first time Marion realized that Tarleton was accompanied not only by cavalry but by his Legion as well. Marion also realized, even before Richardson finished speaking, that the British were undoubtedly already on their way to seize him. His reaction to the news was immediate and based on his usual determination not to risk his men unnecessarily. The order to advance, which he had given just before Richardson's appearance, was replaced by an order to retreat. Without a moment's loss of time Marion led his men at a rapid gallop back toward an almost impassable swamp known as the Woodyard, straight through its watery fastness—along trails that few could have followed even in daylight—and on again for another six miles before he permitted his exhausted mounts to halt.

Tarleton, in the meantime, elated at the thought that Marion was within his grasp, had moved through the trees at a cautious rate, determined to surprise the sentries Marion was known always to post around his camps. His elation turned to fury when he realized that Marion was no longer where he was supposed to have been. With a determination equal to Marion's own, Tarleton then drove his men forward along Marion's trail until he too reached the Woodyard. But one look at the wall-like green growth rising in front of him told Tarleton his cavalrymen and his Legion could not possibly cross that swamp in the dark, and he called a reluctant halt at its edge for the rest of the night.

With the first glimmer of the gray November dawn on the far side of the Woodyard, Marion was on his way again. By now, however, he had decided not to retreat indefinitely, and had chosen the place where he felt he could make a stand even against Tarleton's superior force. A headlong race of thirty-five miles along the Black River brought him to the site he had chosen at Benbow's Ferry, and there Marion prepared to hold off the British. A swamp protected his rear and both flanks. Swiftly felled trees were used to blockade the only trail approaching his front. Marion stationed his best marksmen behind those roadblocks and in the woods alongside the trail, and then calmly settled down to await the man whom Patriots referred to as "Butcher" Tarleton.

But dawn had shown Tarleton that the Woodyard was beyond the tracking skill of his men even in daylight. Furiously he had swung his entire force to one side and led them around the edge of the swamp in the hope of picking up Marion's trail again on its opposite side. For seven hours he drove his cavalry, his supply wagons and his two pieces of artillery at a pace that made his horses drop in their tracks. His officers pleaded with him to halt long enough for the animals to revive, but Tarleton was ruthless. Riders who had lost their mounts were left to trot breathlessly along after their more fortunate fellows, until they too fell exhausted along the way.

Then Tarleton's scouts reported that the route they were following ran head on into another swamp. If there was a trail across it they had been unable to discover any sign of it. Ox Swamp, as it was called, blocked the way around the Woodyard —and the road to Marion—as effectively as a stone wall.

Later, in his own account of the chase, Tarleton said he would have continued it by one route or another, and brought it to a successful conclusion, if a messenger from Cornwallis had not reached him at that moment ordering him back to Winnsboro. There is no doubt that Cornwallis did send for him at approximately that time: Sumter had just badly mauled a force under Wemyss, capturing that commander in the process, and Cornwallis wanted Tarleton to annihilate Sumter's partisans. But it is also probably true that a baffled and enraged Tarleton was glad to set down a reasonable excuse for having failed to catch a maddeningly elusive enemy.

At any rate this was apparently the occasion when Tarleton bestowed on two partisan leaders the names by which they would thereafter be known to generations of admiring Americans.

"Come on, boys. Let's go back. We'll soon find the Gamecock," Tarleton is supposed to have said, referring to Sumter. "But as for this Swamp Fox," he added, "the devil himself could not catch him!"

CHAPTER

XI

Tarleton did find the Gamecock. He attacked the log tobacco warehouse in which Sumter had entrenched himself, was driven back by deadly fire, but took over the warehouse the next morning after Sumter had slipped away in the night. Possession of the building gave Tarleton the chance to call himself victorious in that affair, although he had lost ninety men, with a hundred wounded against three wounded—unfortunately including Sumter himself—and one dead in the Patriot ranks.

But neither Tarleton nor any other British officer could even pretend that he had caught the Swamp Fox. As the year 1780 drew to a close, Francis Marion became an increasing menace in the eyes of the enemy. He was concentrating on the raiding of enemy supply lines, and he could not have chosen a more effective way to use the recently increased strength of his Brigade and his own skill as a strategist.

Supply lines carry the lifeblood of an army fighting in enemy country as England was doing. England might use American Tories as allies and look to Tories for part of the vast amounts of food her forces consumed. Grain and livestock seized on Patriot farms could also help to feed her men and her horses. But most of the military supplies and equipment she used had to be transported across the Atlantic and then carried overland by wagon trains from British-held ports to all her forces stationed at inland posts. Marion was giving his chief attention to the supply line between Charleston and Camden. And he had another purpose in addition to preventing vital supplies from reaching Cornwallis' Camden garrison. He knew that every British or Tory soldier who had to be stationed along the Camden route, in order to protect it—or try to protect it—against partisan raids was a man no longer available for active service elsewhere. So Marion didn't despair over the unusual number of British troops that took up positions along that route. He welcomed their presence.

Marion's harrying of the Camden road began at Charleston itself, where boatmen and draymen secretly friendly to the Patriot cause often picked up vital information which they transmitted to Marion as soon as they left the city. From them Marion learned about British troop transports and supply ships expected in the harbor, and often knew the contents of a supply train before it was loaded for its long trip inland.

He seldom massed his entire Brigade for an attack on such a train. Instead, he divided it into small groups, each trained to operate with lightning speed. The dozen or so men in one of these groups could hide behind cover so scanty that the British would never suspect it of concealing an ambush. They could fire fast and accurately. They could leap into their saddles and make their getaway before their startled victims could retaliate.

Normally such an assault lasted less than five minutes, but its effect was inevitable confusion. An orderly procession of mounted soldiers and horse-drawn vehicles had been transformed by some kind of black magic into complete and churning chaos. Horses were rearing in terror, unseating their riders and upsetting wagons. Or they were bolting panic-stricken into the fields, dragging shattered conveyances behind them and scattering their loads left and right. Restoring order to the convoy again was a job that often took several hours and frequently prevented the supply train from reaching a protected post by nightfall. In such cases the train was usually subjected to a second and even more devastating assault after dark, during which Marion's men could burn or seize and carry away supplies of great value.

Desperately the British tried to figure out where Marion might schedule an ambush, so that the place could be specially guarded. Invariably they proved to be wrong. When they were most certain that Marion had disappeared from a certain area, he might stage two attacks there within a single hour, one many miles distant from the other.

Marion's own intelligence network was an amateur one, but seldom—as in connection with the Tarleton affair—did it make serious mistakes. Marion learned immediately, for example, that the commanders of two British regiments stationed at Nelson's Ferry had determined upon an all-out attack on the Brigade, aided by reinforcements from Charleston to be stationed at Marion's rear in order to cut off his escape into the trackless swamps along the Pee Dee. Marion simply called in all his raiding parties and long before the Charleston reinforcements had arrived and the attack could take place, he was hiding out in the security of Snow Island. He remained there until the elaborate plan for his capture had been reluctantly abandoned.

By the end of 1780 it had become commonplace for the British to send several hundred soldiers along as guards for a supply train on its way to Camden. Marion, much pleased at this strain on British manpower, drew forth another suprise from his bag of partisan tricks. He simply shifted his men temporarily to the job of harassing slow-moving foraging parties burdened down with grain, eggs, firewood, and other provisions, and those foraging parties developed an unhappy habit of not returning to camp. Scouting parties sent out to trace them might return with the alarming reports of dead soldiers stripped of their red coats and of everything else they wore or carried; or the scouting parties, too, might fail to return.

One of Marion's tricks was deliberately to expose himself on a small rise not far from the road the British were traveling. The slight figure mounted on the handsome horse was always an irresistible temptation to enemy officers. They knew they could cover themselves with glory if they could capture the elusive partisan who had so often damaged the self-esteem of England's forces in South Carolina. Time after time one of those officers would leave his convoy and race up the hill with a few cavalrymen to catch the Swamp Fox who had apparently, at long last, delivered himself into the hands of a foe. Not one of those parties ever got within gun range of Marion. Hidden Brigadesmen picked them off as they tore past an innocent-looking bush or boulder. And in the meantime, back on the road, a whole supply train or laden foraging party was being thrown into milling disorder by the rest of Marion's partisans.

Marion's own men were always thoroughly alarmed when he endangered his life by one of these decoy-like performances. They realized, if Marion's modesty prevented him from seeing it himself, that the Brigade would fall to pieces if Marion were killed or captured. But the commander who was always so protective of his men never seemed to recognize the risks he took himself. When Marion did finally give up the role of decoy it was not out of caution; it was simply because that particular trick had ceased to work. Even the most ambitious British or Tory officer finally learned that chasing the Swamp Fox was a fool's game that too often ended in disaster for the pursuer.

Marion had had the unwilling respect of the British for nearly six months before word reached him that George Washington's Continental Army staff was also beginning to recognize his importance. The word came from General Nathanael Greene, who had just been appointed commander of what was left of the Southern Army as a replacement for the ignominiously defeated Gates. A former Quaker, Greene had learned military tactics by poring over textbooks in his Rhode Island blacksmith shop, and had turned against his peaceable Quaker principles to become one of Washington's ablest officers and best strategists. In a letter he wrote to Marion on December 4, the very day he arrived at Charlotte to take over his new command, he showed he was also a competent judge of men.

"I have not the honor of your acquaintance," Greene wrote,

"but am no stranger to your character and merit." Then he went on to prove his ability as a strategist by his appreciation of Marion's skill in that field:

> Your services in the lower part of South Carolina in awing the Tories and preventing the enemy from extending their limits, have been very important. And it is my earnest desire that you continue where you are until farther advice from me . . . I am fully sensible your service is hard and sufferings great, but how great the prize for which we contend! I like your plan of frequently shifting your ground . . . Until a more permanent army can be collected than is in the field at present, we must endeavor to keep up a partisan war, and preserve the tide of sentiment among the people in our favor as much as possible.

Greene concluded the letter with a request for Marion's help in collecting information:

> Spies are the eyes of an army, and without them a general is always groping in the dark, and can neither secure himself, nor annoy his enemy. At present I am badly off for intelligence. It is of the highest importance that I get the earliest intelligence of any reinforcement which may arrive in Charleston . . .

Marion already had news to send up to Greene—the information that Major General Alexander Leslie had arrived at Charleston with over two thousand men to reinforce England's South Carolina garrisons. Some fifteen hundred of these troops were already on their way to Winnsboro to inject new blood into Cornwallis' army there.

It was not a very cheering bulletin, of course, for the new American commander. Greene realized that Cornwallis would probably soon be ready once more to try a march northward, and was at the moment unable to make any preventive move against such a march. He would need more than information before he could do that. He would also need food and ammunition—two commodities he desperately lacked. Again he appealed to Marion. And from his partisan headquarters on Snow Island, on the next to the last day of 1780, Marion issued the first of a series of brisk orders designed to secure those supplies.

The orders, in effect, imposed a kind of American martial law on the district in which Marion operated—a countermeasure to the British martial law under which Carolina had been suffering for months. They were issued with the authority of a general, an authority Marion had seldom displayed so openly. Major John Postell, a Brigade officer who had already led successful raiding and foraging parties, received a typical example of these new orders:

Snow's Island, Dec. 30, 1780

Sir,

You will proceed with a party down Black River, from Black Mingo to the Mouth of the Pee Dee, and come up to this place; you will take all the boats and canoes from Euhaney up, and impress negroes to bring them to camp; put some men to see them safe; you will take every horse, to whomsoever he may belong, whether friend or foe. You will take all arms and ammunition for the use of our service. You will forbid all persons from carrying any grains, stock or any sort of provision for Georgetown, or where the enemy may get them, on the pain of being held as traitors and enemies to the Americans. All persons who will not join you you will take prisoners and bring to me. You will return as soon as possible. Let me know any intelligence you may gain of the enemy's strength or movements.

I am, your obedient servant,
Francis Marion

N.B. You will bring up as much rice and salt in the boats as possible.

Within a matter of days Postell and other officers were conducting raids in a dozen different directions. Many of them were remarkably successful. But Greene had an army of two thousand men, all of them hungry and most of them weaponless, and Marion realized that even the most successful small-scale foraging expeditions would not furnish that army with the quantity of supplies it needed. He began seriously, for the first time, to contemplate a raid on Georgetown.

That busy little port was no less well protected then than it had been in the past, and always in the past Marion had refused to risk his Brigade in an assault against its stockade and fortifications. But Georgetown was the storage center for a large supply of munitions, clothing, medical supplies and food, and the desperate needs of the moment led Marion to hope that his partisans could obtain some of these stores without making an all-out attack. If his men could get inside the fortifications, for example, by means of a sudden drive against one gate, they might be able to overpower the arsenal and warehouse guards in a hand-to-hand combat and escape with valuable supplies before a full-scale engagement could develop. Marion decided to make the attempt.

Early in January in the new year, 1781, he marched coastward at the head of a sizable force. When he was within three miles of Georgetown he hid his men in a swamp to await the reports of two scouting parties, one led by Peter Horry and the other by John Melton. Marion's young nephew Gabriel volunteered to go out with Melton's group. After dusk the scouts took up positions in the woods at the very edge of the town. Their orders were to watch the British throughout the following day and rejoin the Brigade at nightfall.

But enemy patrols discovered both parties early in the morning. Horry routed the Dragoons that attacked him. Melton was less fortunate when he found himself surprised by a large group of Tories.

In the wild melee that followed, one of the Tories shot Gabriel Marion's horse out from under him. Another, recognizing the youthful soldier as a kinsman of the hated Swamp Fox, put his pistol against Gabriel's chest and killed him on the spot. When Melton and the rest of the party escaped a few minutes later by superb horsemanship and hard riding, they had to leave the lifeless young body behind them.

The possibility of surprising Georgetown had been lost. Discovery of the scouting parties meant that the proposed attack must be abandoned. But the men who marched back to Snow Island, behind a silent and tight-lipped general, were more enraged over the cold-blooded murder of Gabriel Marion than over the failure of their raid. Talking quietly among themselves, they swore to revenge the death of the young man who had held such a warm place in his uncle's affections.

Not many days after the retreat from Georgetown, a party under Peter Horry captured a group of Tories among whom—according to a member of that ill-fated scouting party—was the culprit they sought. Horry, sensing immediately the new trigger-like temper of his men doubled the guard around the prisoners and reminded his followers of Marion's strict orders against vengeance killings. The precautions were futile. After dark a mounted man raced along the column, paused briefly beside the prisoners, fired a single shot into the group, and vanished. The man he had aimed at was dead.

Horry halted the column and questioned every man in it. They all declared the assailant had been a stranger—that he was not, as Horry was sure, one of themselves. Marion asked questions too, on the party's return to camp, with the same results.

Marion's men were quietly triumphant, and Marion knew better than to press them. The matter was dropped.

In the meantime, refusing to permit himself the luxury of grief for his nephew's death, Marion had already begun to plan another attack on Georgetown. Having decided that his own Brigade was not strong enough to guarantee success on such a venture, he had written to Greene asking that reinforcements—preferably Continentals trained in the use of the bayonet—be loaned to him for the purpose. But because Sumter was still convalescing from the wound he had received in his engagement with Tarleton, Marion's Brigade was the only partisan force operating in the state. So while he awaited a reply from Greene, he continued to send out raiding parties under Postell, Horry and other officers.

On one of these forays Postell proved as selfless as his commander. He received intelligence that British grenadiers were quartered in his father's house, and promptly surrounded the building with the shouted warning that he would burn it down around them unless they surrendered. The British, certain that no man would destroy his own home, disregarded the demand. Postell then managed to get into the kitchen, actually started a conflagration there—and calmly accepted the surrender of the amazed redcoats when they found themselves threatened by billowing smoke and leaping flames.

Horry distinguished himself in several raids at this time too, although not always in the manner he had planned. Previously an infantry commander, and a very fine one, he had recently persuaded Marion to give him command of some sixty cavalrymen because, as Horry himself admitted, a horse would give him added distinction and permit him to cut a more dashing figure with the ladies. But Horry was a poor horseman, and his new men were mostly raw recruits. "Half-made new Whigs," Horry called them.

In one of their first sallies together against the enemy, one of Horry's men, sent ahead on a scouting mission, failed to recognize the sound of a British bugler's signal for a cavalry charge. Mistaking it for a hunting call instead, he cheerfully advised the five men with him to stop where they were so that they could enjoy the sight of "deer, dogs and huntsman as they cross the road." The redcoated "huntsmen" who appeared the next instant were not the kind he had innocently expected, and Horry's main party rode up barely in time to rescue the bungling soldiers from a determined assault by British dragoons. Then, a moment later, Horry's mount threw him and bolted, and Horry, standing bewildered there in the road, became aware that he too had made a mistake. Too late he realized that the dragoons his men were fighting were merely the advance guard of the large company of British infantry suddenly appearing on the run. The inexperienced Patriot cavalry took one look at the approaching forest of flashing bayonets, turned their mounts and fled. If Horry had not been picked up bodily and thrust onto the horse of a faithful follower, his terrified men would have escaped without him. Their retreat that day was a shameful rout.

But Horry and his company redeemed themselves not long afterward. Riding along the Sampit River road, daringly close to Georgetown, they spotted a group of Tories slaughtering cattle for the British garrison in the town. Horry attacked instantly, before the Tories could drop their work and prepare to defend themselves. This time his men fought bravely throughout an entire morning, unflagging in their zeal even when a second Tory party arrived to join the battle, led by the same Major Gainey who had been the first victim of Marion's Brigade.

Finally the Tories had had enough. They scattered into the nearby woods or pounded away down the road leading to the haven at Georgetown. But another glory was still to be added to the day.

Sergeant McDonald, one of the three Continentals who had joined the Brigade when Marion rescued the hundred and fifty prisoners at Nelson's Ferry, suddenly decided that Gainey, at least, should not be permitted to escape. Digging heels into his horse's flanks, he took off after the Tory as fast as his animal could gallop. Gainey's companion bravely fell back to intercept his commander's pursuer and McDonald cut him down with a single shot. Closer and closer he drew to his quarry. At last his horse's head was even with the streaming tail of Gainey's mount, and McDonald lunged forward and thrust his bayonet into Gainey's back. The partisan's horse faltered under the force of the blow, and the blade ripped loose from the musket. It was still protruding from the Tory's back as Gainey raced on into town. McDonald never saw the weapon again. But his lost bayonet inspired a lively legend that helped win lasting fame for Horry's company and the men of Marion's Brigade.

Even dramatically successful, legend-inspiring raids, however —unless they were much larger than those the Brigade had been conducting—couldn't provide the huge amounts of materièl Greene needed in order to face Cornwallis on anything like equal terms. Greene knew that himself and was making up his mind to send Marion reinforcements for another attempt on the storehouses of Georgetown.

Greene had far fewer men than the total number of British troops Cornwallis had distributed among his posts at Ninety-

Six, Winnsboro and Camden. Another commander in Greene's place might therefore have refused to dispatch part of his force on a raiding expedition several hundred miles from his base. But Greene was an unorthodox general, as he had already proved by the disposition he had made of his small army. In defiance of the accepted rules of warfare he had divided it into two sections. One, under General Dan Morgan, the "Old Wagoner," was encamped west of Winnsboro at a point that formed a triangle with that British garrison and the one at Ninety-Six. The second force, under Greene himself, was located on the opposite side of Winnsboro, to form a second triangle with that place and Camden.

If Cornwallis was really determined to march northward again, Greene knew he couldn't stop him. Cornwallis could attack either of the little Patriot forces, and the other would not be able to come to its rescue. And if Cornwallis defeated them both, his way would be open clear to Virginia. But Greene was gambling on two factors: the ability of his army to outrun the British if necessary; and the British general's confusion when faced by an unusual situation. And Greene soon realized that, so far as Cornwallis was concerned, he had guessed correctly. Certain that a man of Greene's ability would not invite open disaster by splitting an inferior force into two parts, Cornwallis had made the mistaken assumption that the American must be expecting reinforcements momentarily. Consequently Cornwallis had not attacked and clearly didn't intend to until Greene's reinforcements arrived and Cornwallis could judge of their strength.

The moment Greene was certain of Cornwallis' hesitance, he seized the breathing space the Englishman had offered him and sent part of his force to Marion, not only to aid the partisan in an attack on Georgetown but also to join him in another project Greene regarded of equal importance: the destruction of a force of five hundred Tories stationed at Nelson's Ferry but likely to join Cornwallis at any moment.

The men Greene sent to Marion were the best-equipped, best-trained and best-disciplined soldiers in his command—perhaps the best in the entire American army at that time. Half cavalry, half infantry, they made up the remarkably mobile Legion of Colonel Henry Lee, the famous Light Horse Harry Lee of Virginia.

To send Lee and his Legion to Marion, to put them in effect under his orders, was perhaps the finest compliment Greene could pay to the partisan of South Carolina. It was active proof that Marion's gallant efforts for the Patriot cause had definitely won the respect of his own superiors, as they had long before won the fearful respect of his enemies.

CHAPTER

XII

Colonel Light Horse Harry Lee of Virginia was about as different from Marion as a man could possibly be. Dashing, handsome, well educated, talented in many fields, Lee was fond of good living and of gaiety. He talked easily and wittily and enjoyed an audience. But, like Marion, he was an excellent raider and skilled in making rapid, slashing attacks on unsuspecting enemies.

Expert as Lee was, however, he couldn't find Marion after reaching the Pee Dee where he had expected to rendezvous with the partisan. He might never have found Marion at all except for accidentally discovering, through friends, a small foraging party of the Brigade. The foragers took Lee to their general, "who had changed his ground since the party left him," Lee wrote in his *Memoirs*, "which occasioned many hours search even before his own men could find him."

Perhaps it was this magnificent proof of Marion's elusiveness that impressed Lee. Perhaps he simply learned to admire the South Carolinian after they had seen service together. In any any event, Lee's opinion of Marion was extremely high.

> His visage [Lee wrote] was not pleasing, and his manners not captivating. He was reserved and silent, entering into conversation only when necessary, and then with modesty and good sense. He possessed a strong mind, improved by its own reflections and observations, not by books or travel. His dress was like his address—

plain, regarding comfort and decency only. In his meals he was abstemious, eating generally of one dish, and drinking water mostly ... Even the charms of the fair, like the luxuries of the table and the allurements of wealth, seemed to be lost on him ... Enthusiastically wedded to the cause of liberty, he deeply deplored the doleful condition of his beloved country. The common weal was his sole object; nothing selfish, nothing mercenary soiled his ermine character ... A rigid disciplinarian, he reduced to practice the justice of his heart; and during the difficult course of warfare through which he passed, calumny itself never charged him with molesting the rights of person, property or humanity ...

These two men, both utterly devoted to the cause for which they fought, were unwilling to let a single day go by without trying to advance that cause. Lee arrived in Marion's camp on January 23, and early the following evening Lee's Legion and Marion's Brigade were already moving out toward Georgetown for an attack that Marion had previously planned in careful detail.

Lee's men were handsome in their short green jackets and yellow breeches. Marion's volunteers, as usual, wore confiscated British coats—dyed into a nondescript color—or shabby remnants of their own civilian garments. But there was a camaraderie among the men, as there was respect between the two leaders. Lee had trained his Legionaires, as Marion had trained the members of his Brigade, to travel swiftly in difficult country, to attack hard and suddenly, and to retreat, if necessary, with all speed. The venture ahead of the two united forces seemed to promise almost certain success.

Their approach to Georgetown was made by two routes, one by water, one by land. Lee's infantrymen, commanded by two captains, Patrick Carnes and Michael Rudulph, were ferried down the Pee Dee in boats piloted by some of Marion's men. Lee's cavalry and Marion's mounted partisans rode toward their goal by hidden trails. By midnight the next night both parties had taken up the positions assigned to them. Carnes and Rudulph were hidden with their men on a marshy island near the Pee Dee's mouth on Winyah Bay and separated from the rear of Georgetown only by a few miles of watery rice field, which the British confidently believed to be impassable. Marion and Lee were concealed on the opposite side of the town, ready to join in the attack that Carnes and Rudulph were to open.

Between one and two o'clock in the morning the boats that had traveled down the Pee Dee were launched again, and Carnes and Rudulph's men were poled through the rice fields and around to the rear of the town. Ahead of them, in the dark, lay the defenses they would have to overcome: several small positions manned by about two hundred soldiers under the command of the British Lieutenant Colonel George Campbell, and a fort in which only a few soldiers were normally stationed. Most of the redcoats on daily duty at the fort slept outside its walls, quartered in houses nearby.

Carnes and Rudulph landed their men so quietly that the enemy had no warning of their approach. Carnes immediately led his men to the house where Campbell lived, took it without difficulty and captured Campbell and several of his aides in short order. But Rudulph, assigned the task of marching upon the open and almost deserted fort and seizing it before the British could rally to its defense, failed to reach the stockade in time. The noise of Carnes' attack had alerted the garrison, and a force of soldiers had rushed into the fort and barricaded its heavy doors before Rudulph could reach them. The Americans had no storming equipment with which to attack the heavy log walls. They were helpless. Marion and Lee, galloping up a few minutes later, were equally helpless without artillery and scaling ladders.

Marion could make only one decision. If the Patriots remained outside the fort until daybreak they would then form perfect targets not only for the fort's cannon and its defending musketmen but also for the many British soldiers who were barricaded behind the stout walls of their quarters, ready to fire as soon as it was light. With Lee's concurrence, therefore, Marion paroled Colonel Campbell and his aides, and withdrew the Brigade and the Legion before the first streaks of dawn paled the sky.

The two commanders permitted their men no time to indulge in regrets over the lack of success at Georgetown. Another task still lay ahead of them and it would require all their energy. The Tories whom General Greene wanted them to engage at Nelson's Ferry were as numerous as the Patriot force now moving against them, and well entrenched besides, with two pieces of light artillery. At Nelson's Ferry, as at Georgetown, surprise could be the only real weapon in the American's arsenal, and surprise demanded a swift march.

But again, as at Georgetown, the thrust of surprise was blunted into uselessness. Colonel John Watson, commander of Fort Watson, just above the ferry, was warned by Tory spies of Marion's approach. He reacted in a manner that was flattering to Marion and that was good military tactics as well. He fled from the fort and headed toward Camden. But by leaving his cannon in the fort, together with artillerymen and a fair body of regular soldiers, he deprived the Patriots of even the slight satisfaction of seizing the fort itself. And by joining one of Cornwallis' inland garrisons, Watson made precisely the move that Greene hoped Marion and Lee could prevent.

Marion and Lee, riding soberly back to Snow Island, were faced with the disagreeable task of reporting double failure to Greene. But before their dispatch could reach him, they received news from Greene's headquarters that made their own seem trivial in contrast.

The apparent stalemate between a confused Cornwallis and a wily Greene had unexpectedly exploded into activity. Greene's second in command, the "Old Wagoner" Dan Morgan, had provoked the explosion. His cavalry, under young Colonel William Washington, had fallen on a force of over two hundred Tories, captured forty of them and killed and wounded most of the rest. Then, without firing a shot, they had captured a British outpost within fifteen miles of the powerful fort at Ninety-Six. Cornwallis, aware that the Americans would penetrate all the way into Georgia if he did not take immediate action against them, sent Tarleton after Morgan with a force of a thousand men, including infantry, cavalry and even artillery.

Morgan had promptly begun an orderly retreat, marching northward for two days until he reached the Broad River near the North Carolina border. There he halted his men at a cluster of cow pens maintained for the use of cattle owners driving their beasts eastward to market. And there, at Cowpens, as it was called, against Greene's firm instructions to avoid an engagement, Morgan had turned to face his pursuers. The battle that followed was one of the most dramatic and most important of the Revolution. Morgan knew the nervousness of his raw militia recruits and suspected that they might break and run in terror at the first sight of British bayonets. But he hadn't warned them not to retreat: he actually told them they could—after waiting until the enemy came into range and firing two volleys. Those two volleys had been brutally effective because Morgan also knew the British habit of a reckless, head-on assault whenever they faced militiamen. Morgan then let the staggered British further exhaust themselves chasing up the slope of a hill, to be met at the top by a devastating rifle and bayonet attack from fresh Continental troops in hiding there. As the bewildered redcoats reeled back from that blow, they had been struck hard on one flank by Washington's cavalry and on the other by the militia, now newly confident.

The famous "Butcher" Tarleton had scarcely become aware of danger when he found himself tearing off in a wild retreat with only a handful of his once-proud men. Behind him the "Old Wagoner" was triumphantly rounding up six hundred captives and counting a hundred British dead and two hundred wounded. He had also taken Tarleton's light artillery, eight hundred of his muskets, thirty-five supply wagons and a hundred cavalry horses—all at a price of only twelve Patriot dead and sixty-one wounded.

The amazing battle of Cowpens had taken place on January 17, a week before Greene had sent Lee off to join Morgan, but

Greene hadn't learned of it until Lee had gone. He dispatched the good news to Marion on January 23. Only a few days later a far less cheerful message reached the partisans' camp: Lee and his Legion were ordered to rejoin Greene immediately. Both halves of Greene's army were already racing desperately northward along paths that would reunite them eventually. A furiously vengeful Cornwallis was hard on their heels. Greene's hopes had been reduced to the single desire of reaching Virginia with his force intact and there finding temporary safety.

Lee and his Legion left Marion's camp without a moment's delay.

Once more, against the background of his own two failures, and the knowledge of Greene's enforced retreat, Marion was left practically alone to defend the Patriot cause in South Carolina.

Lee once wrote of Marion that the Brigade commander was "never elated with prosperity, nor depressed with adversity," and that throughout the long and difficult years of the war he "preserved an equanimity which won the admiration of his friends and exalted the respect of his enemies." Now, in the grim winter of 1781, Marion was illustrating the truth of those words. Beset on every side by adversity, he apparently still did not doubt the Patriots' ultimate success and calmly each day made whatever efforts were within his power toward that success.

The constant lengthening of Cornwallis' lines of communication, as his army raced north, gave Marion's highly skilled raiders ideal opportunities for causing mischief. Again he divided his Brigade into small groups and set them in motion in many directions. An order issued January 29, 1781, to John Postell is typical of those that sent Postell and his brother James, the Horry brothers, and various other Brigade officers out into the night through the swamps:

> Dear Sir:
> You will cross the Santee River with twenty-five men, and make a forced march to Wadboo bridge, there burn all the British stores of every kind . . . You will return the same way, and recross the

river at the same place, which must be done before daylight next morning. After effecting my purpose at Wadboo, it will not be out of your way to come by Monck's Corner, and destroy any stores or waggons you may find there. You can learn from the people at Wadboo what guard there is at the corner; if it should be too strong you will not attempt that place . . . The destruction of all British stores in the above-mentioned places is of the greatest consequence to us, and only requires boldness and expedition. Take care that your men do not get at liquor, or clog themselves with plunder so as to endanger their retreat.

I am with regard, dear Sir,
Your obedient servant,
Francis Marion

While his brother James was routing a British guard and setting fire to a huge store of British supplies at a place called Manigault's Ferry, John Postell was brilliantly carrying out his assignment at Wadboo and racing for Monck's Corner while the fires he had set were still lighting the night sky. At Monck's Corner he surrounded a guarded supply train, captured thirty-five men, scattered the rest and seized eleven wagons loaded with clothing, blankets and other equipment. Some of the captured loot was used to replenish the tattered wardrobes of Marion's men. The rest was sold and the proceeds divided among the raiders. The value of paper money had fallen very low by then. The partisans received twenty-two hundred nearly worthless Continental dollars for a blanket, sold a coat for six thousand two hundred and ten dollars, and a pair of stockings for eight hundred dollars. But to unpaid volunteers who had seen no money at all for many months, the paper bills they earned from the seized British goods were a welcome sight. They complained bitterly when those two swift raids on Wadboo and Monck's Corner proved to be among the last Postell conducted. Very shortly afterward, while on a visit to Georgetown under a flag of truce to arrange for an exchange of prisoners, Postell was seized and arrested by the British for having broken his parole.

Marion had been reluctant to let Postell take on that exchange assignment because he feared the British might do just what they did. But the officer himself, eager to see his aged father then imprisoned in Georgetown, had been sure he would be safe under a flag of truce. It was true that, like many of the partisans, he had broken the pledge of neutrality demanded of him earlier in the war. But in Postell's own opinion the British could not legally condemn him for that, because they had previously seized his property which, as a parolee, he had expected them to protect.

Busy as he was, Marion found the time to maintain a correspondence with the enemy about Postell's case. He threatened retaliation and even held as a hostage a British officer who had come into his own camp under a white flag. Marion's anger and threats probably kept the British from carrying out their avowed intention of hanging Postell. But nothing Marion did could affect the young officer's release and Postell remained in prison for the entire duration of the war.

In early February, Marion conducted a large raid that the several hundred men with him long remembered as one of the most curious in their military experience.

In the beginning it followed a familiar enough pattern. The Swamp Fox had learned that a large British supply train, then at Nelson's Ferry, was about to set out for the northwest under guard of several hundred infantrymen commanded by a Major McLeroth. Marion set his ambush some twenty miles from the convoy's starting point—far enough away from the ferry so that McLeroth could not obtain quick help from there when he found himself under attack.

Marion let almost the entire supply train move past the point where he and his men were hidden in the woods. Not until the rear guard appeared did he sweep out onto the road, demolishing the guard with one swift blow and vanishing again. While the disrupted train was being reorganized, Marion led his men a few miles further along the road and set another ambush. This time he struck a double blow, attacking both the vanguard and the rear guard simultaneously.

McLeroth, realizing that his entire force would shortly be

totally destroyed by its invisible enemies, held to the road for only another mile, during which his men fired steadily into the underbrush as they raced along. As soon as he found an open field, McLeroth moved his whole train into it and prepared for outright battle, for the kind of fighting in which his soldiers would be at less of a disadvantage. When Marion caught up with him, the Brigade commander took up a position on the other side of the road, several hundred yards from the British, and awaited the enemy's next move.

But McLeroth did not attack, as Marion expected him to. Instead he sent an officer to the partisan under a flag of truce, challenging Marion—surprisingly—to personal combat in full view of both their forces.

The unusual suggestion could hardly have appealed to Marion. He had never been a warrior of the swashbuckling type, eager to display his own prowess. He regarded McLeroth's suggestion as the offer of a desperate man and not to be taken seriously. But if McLeroth preferred a small engagement to a full-scale battle in order to save lives, Marion was willing, he said, to pit twenty of his men against twenty British.

American marksmanship was known to be superior to that of the redcoats. Marion was thus surprised again when McLeroth accepted this counteroffer. For the next several hours both sides prepared for the combat and set its pattern in agreements exchanged between the two commanders. Each group of twenty men was to march out into an open field, swing around to face their opponents, and fire at will. Finally the signal was given and the representatives of both sides started forward.

But when the redcoats were still a hundred yards away from the Americans—twice the distance at which the partisans planned to fire their first volley—a British officer raced out to speak to them, and they immediately turned and marched back to McLeroth and his main force.

The amazed Patriots waited for them to reappear. Nothing further happened. And since the day was by then drawing to a close, they started to make camp, keeping a watchful eye on the enemy. The British made camp too, and soon their fires were all that could be seen of them.

In the morning McLeroth was gone. Apparently his suggestion of a personal combat, followed by his apparent acceptance of Marion's plan, had both been ruses to avoid any real combat with the Brigade. McLeroth had simply piled his fires high enough to burn through the night, and slipped quietly away behind their misleading glow.

Marion sent Horry after the fleeing British with a hundred fast horsemen, while the rest of the Brigade gathered up the wealth of supplies McLeroth had had to leave behind. Horry soon realized that McLeroth was heading for a mill owned by the Singleton family, and dispatched his fleetest riders, under Major James, to that place. James, cutting through woods and swamps, reached it before the British did. But there was smallpox among the Singletons, and the partisans refused to use the infected building as a protective stronghold from which to ambush the approaching enemy. James withdrew to a safe distance and halted his men to watch. When McLeroth arrived, he proved once more that the Swamp Fox's reputation had frightened him out of the will to fight. He led his men straight into the mill and barricaded them there, deliberately risking smallpox in preference to the greater danger of Marion's men. James rode away content with the knowledge that though McLeroth was still undefeated, the Brigade had accomplished its purpose of stopping the supplies from reaching Cornwallis.

Most British officers by that time probably shared McLeroth's reluctance to tangle with Marion, but the British high command was determined that the Swamp Fox must somehow be run to earth. By mid-February Greene's army of two thousand had been chased as far north as Virginia, and it was galling to His Majesty's officers to have to admit that lesser partisan bands were still at large in South Carolina. Sumter had at last recovered from the wound inflicted on him by Tarleton's men, and was again conducting guerrilla warfare in the western part of the colony, Marion was terrorizing the Tories and the British garrisons in the eastern areas. Elaborate plans were made to destroy both bands once and for all. Not long after the curious McLeroth affair some of Marion's scouts hurried back to Snow Island with the news that Colonel Watson—the man who had fled Fort Watson on the Brigade's approach there in company with Lee's Legion—was on his way with light artillery, five hundred men and the announced purpose of finding and destroying Marion's headquarters.

Marion promptly called in all his scouts and raiding parties and set forth to meet this formidable enemy. He arranged his first ambush for Watson at a place called Wiboo Swamp, in what is now Clarendon County, some fifty miles inland from Charleston.

A party of crack riflemen under Peter Horry, hidden in the shelter of the swamp, let loose the first fire when Watson's advance cavalry appeared. The horsemen broke and ran. Watson quickly set up his artillery and poured a shower of grapeshot into the trees that concealed his unseen assailants. Horry's men fled noisily, as if in utter panic, and Watson sent his vengeful cavalry after them, under Major Harrison, one of the ill-famed Tory brothers.

But Marion had signaled that retreat for a deliberate purpose. As the Tories dashed into the dank, moss-hung woods, a party of Brigade horsemen slammed into their flank and the forest shadows suddenly came alive with flashing, thrusting blades. Young Captain Daniel Conyers, one of Marion's officers, hacked his way through the melee to Harrison and cut him down in an instant. Then Marion sent a second partisan unit into the miniature battle raging among the trees, and the badly worsted Tories were driven back in a rout to the safety of Watson's artillery-protected main force.

Watson had to make camp on the open grounds of a large plantation nearby to bury his dead and arrange for sending his wounded out of camp.

Several days later, when the redcoat commander resumed his march toward Snow Island, Marion was apparently retreating just ahead of him. Confidently Watson followed, down along the Santee and then off at an angle toward the northeast where the Swamp Fox's headquarters lay. Actually Marion was moving just fast enough to keep out of range of Watson's guns. Every time he came to a bridge he stopped long enough to destroy it. Every time the trail became a narrow causeway through a swamp, Marion's men felled trees across it before they went on.

Watson could tell himself that he was pursuing a fleeing Marion, but he was learning, as other British officers had, that chasing Marion was a nightmare business. Whenever his own men stopped to repair a bridge or tear down a hastily erected barricade of trees, the woods on either side crackled with sudden fire and more of his men fell. Usually they were seriously, if not fatally, wounded. Marion's partisans had started after Watson with only twenty rounds of ammunition apiece, and they were wasting as few of them as possible.

Within a few days Watson's men had grown so nervous and jittery that he changed his plans, hoping at the same time to outwit the Swamp Fox. Instead of swinging left on a road leading toward Snow Island, Watson continued to follow the general direction of the Santee as if he were heading for Georgetown. Then Watson turned left on another road, with a burst of speed calculated to get his men across the Black River before Marion could discover the ruse and get ahead of him to destroy the bridge.

But Marion was keeping such a close watch on the enemy that the trick didn't work. The moment he knew Watson had turned left, he sent Major James and forty cavalrymen, and Captain William McCottry with thirty mounted riflemen, on a quick dash through wild, trackless country to that bridge. They reached it in plenty of time to rip up its planking and set fire to the heavy spanning timbers before Watson arrived. Marion and the rest of the Brigade joined them there a little later, having taken a longer, curving route that permitted them to cross the river at a shallow spot several miles below the bridge.

The partisans had taken an excellent position. Their own northern bank of the river was low and afforded good cover. But the redcoats could reach the southern bank only by descending a high hill, and if they wished to ford the fifty-yard-wide stream, they would have to do it under constant fire. They would even make first-rate targets as they came down the slope before they so much as entered the river.

Watson, furious at the failure of his trick, set up his two small cannon behind the crest of the hill overlooking the stream. He intended to sweep the partisans out of their leafy hiding places by showers of grapeshot. But his cannon, aimed up and over the hilltop, merely whipped at tree branches well over the heads of Marion's men. Watson ordered the guns moved up to the crest itself so that they could be aimed downward directly at the enemy.

Marion's men picked off the gunners in the very act of stepping forward to fire.

Angrily Watson ordered more gunners to the job, cautioning them to work swiftly before the partisans could draw a bead. The caution was useless. The instant the redcoats raised their heads high enough to aim the cannon, those deadly lead balls were flying across the river again on their unerring course. The skill of Marion's riflemen made those cannon as ineffectual as so much scrap metal.

Watson pulled the cannon back out of sight and considered his next move. Unless he retreated immediately, he clearly had only one alternative: to ford the river in the face of the partisans' fire. Swiftly he organized his men into columns and sent the van forward down that exposed hillside.

Captain McCottry and his riflemen watched the redcoats move bravely toward the water. McCottry's own rifle was trained on the officer at their head, his sights lined up on one of the bright buttons of the handsome uniform. Each of his men picked his own target. But McCottry told them to hold their fire until he gave the signal. He waited until that button came within a hundred yards. Then he gently squeezed the trigger. The British officer crumpled to the ground as thirty other rifles cracked. The remnants of the British column broke and ran back up over the hill. That night they picked up their dead and wounded and fell back to an open field a mile away.

Marion set scouts to ranging up and down the river to make certain Watson was not planning a crossing at any other place, while he kept the bulk of his men encamped at a point from which they could watch the old bridge site where Watson was most likely to attempt to ford the stream. He also sent out men skilled at ambush to pick off Watson's own scouting parties and to snipe at his pickets.

Watson soon moved to what seemed a safer position. Three hundred yards of completely treeless open space surrounded his camp. But Sergeant McDonald, who had left his bayonet in Gainey's redcoated back, took careful aim, one day, and shattered the knee of a British lieutenant across even that great distance. Thereafter every enemy soldier was afraid to expose himself in daylight. The nights were even more dangerous. Each one meant the mysterious loss of a guard or two, or a surprise cavalry raid that might do little damage but left Watson's men in a still more shaken state. Their camp became a booby-trapped prison—but to leave it was fatal. Assignment to a foraging party—and such parties had to go out regularly to prevent complete starvation—amounted to an almost certain death warrant.

Watson admitted his helplessness when he had to ask Marion to grant a pass to a party assigned to transport wounded to Charleston. Already his force was so depleted that it was said he sank the bodies of his dead in the Black River after dark in order to conceal the number of burials from the partisans' ever-watchful eyes. Finally, at the end of ten days, Watson gave up. He ordered what was left of his terrified men to break camp and make a dash along the Black River Road to the safety of Georgetown.

But Marion had anticipated even that move. His men had blocked the causeway at the point where the Georgetown road led through Ox Swamp, and had destroyed three bridges. Watson had to shift his course and head south for the Santee River Road.

Unwearied, Marion drove after him. At almost every bend he placed concealed snipers to fire at Watson's front and rear detachments.

Watson's infantry were soon literally running, pounding breathlessly along the road on stamina conjured out of sheer terror. Not until they were within nine miles of Georgetown did Marion's Brigade at last withdraw and leave the remnants of Watson's force to stagger panting into the haven of the British garrison there.

Marion had taught Watson a bitter lesson in partisan warfare. How much the British officer paid for that instruction is not known, but certainly he lost heavily in dead and wounded and more heavily in morale. Marion's own casualties have not been recorded either, but he is believed to have lost just one man during the half-month of constant, remorseless guerrilla fighting.

The punishment meted out to Watson's army did, however, cost Marion high in ammunition. His Brigade had only two bullets per man left, and barely enough powder to fire them. So when Marion turned his back on the fleeing British, he headed straight for Snow Island to replenish his stores and allow his men a brief rest before undertaking another foray against the enemy.

He was on his way there when he learned—as he might have learned much earlier if he hadn't called in all his scouts for the Watson affair—that there was another sizable force from Camden, under Colonel John Doyle, somewhere along the Lynches River not far from Snow Island. Marion decided to tackle this new threat immediately, despite his scanty supply of ammunition. A few days later he was pushing up to a camp that Doyle had obviously left only a short time before—and left without his supplies, as heaps of still warm ashes proved. By questioning the people in the neighborhood Marion discovered that Doyle was racing for Camden as fast as he could go.

But these same people also gave Marion another piece of information which put Doyle's flight in a new and entirely different light. It was undoubtedly true that the redcoats had sacrificed their supplies in order to get back to Camden as quickly as possible. But they had previously taken their vengeance on the Brigade as no other British force had ever been able to do. Doyle and his men had found the camp at Snow Island and had completely destroyed it.

At first the news seemed unbelievable, but investigation proved that it was only too true. There had, of course, not been much to destroy—no barracks, no hospital (Marion's Brigade never had a doctor), no stockades, no mounted artillery. But there had been supplies, and their loss was catastrophic. And there had always been in the past the feeling that Snow Island was a safe haven. Now the knowledge that it had been violated was shocking and unsettling to the members of the Brigade.

Marion was face to face with what was perhaps the blackest moment in his career. His Brigade still numbered five hundred men, and they were still comparatively unwearied even after their ceaseless harassment of Watson and their chase after Doyle. But they had less than a thousand rounds of ammunition among them, and there seemed little immediate hope of obtaining any more. Furthermore, Marion's intelligence service, now in operation again, soon added one more bulletin to the already staggering news the Swamp Fox had received. Watson was on the move again, with nine hundred men freshly equipped from the Georgetown storehouses, and with the firm intention of defeating the man who had driven him into such shameful retreat.

Marion could not fight Watson without ammunition. He refused to waste the strength of his men on an aimless race through the countryside, to keep out of Watson's reach. Reluctantly but decisively, the Swamp Fox ordered his Brigade to disband. He told the men in the ranks to return to their homes by safe and hidden trails, while he and his officers once more retreated into North Carolina to await some future moment when they could renew the struggle in their own state.

The order brought to a close many months of brilliant fighting. Marion was even quieter than usual as he watched his disheartened men slip away into the forest. Some were cheering themselves with the reminder that now, at least, they could do some spring planting. But each one knew, as he said a last good-by to Marion, that the Brigade might never be called together again—that the British grip on South Carolina might now be permanent and unshakable.

Young Captain Gavin Witherspoon, one of Marion's most devoted followers, was seated near the campfire one night, glumly awaiting his commander's orders to prepare for the march north. The Brigade had already shrunk to eighty men. Before the next day was out it would be reduced even closer to the tiny core that would accompany Marion. But when an old man named Baker Johnson wandered into view and announced that he was hungry, Witherspoon politely found him a pot of cold rice. Johnson, a confirmed Patriot, had supplied the Brigade with valuable information in the past, and though the food supply of the little temporary encampment was pitifully low, Johnson was always welcome to share what there was.

Between bites the old man muttered. "Fine news. I saw a great number of Continental troops—horse and foot—crossing at Long Bluff."

Witherspoon leaped to his feet. Continental troops! It seemed impossible. Greene had weeks before reached the safety of Virginia with the whole Southern Army, and Virginia was hundreds of miles away. But Baker Johnson had never been wrong before.

"Come tell the General!" Witherspoon said.

Johnson refused to move. He was starving, he said, and would not budge from the fire until he had eaten every grain of rice. "If the General wants the news he must come to me," he mumbled.

So Witherspoon hurried to Marion's makeshift tent, brought

him to the campfire, and made Johnson repeat his amazing bulletin. Even on second hearing it still seemed incredible.

But even before the independent old Patriot had finished his pot of rice, the news he brought was dramatically confirmed. The startled men around the campfire heard the voices of their own pickets raised in loud challenge. Then the rattle of weapons and the sound of horses' hoofs echoed noisily through the night. A moment later a small troop of horsemen in green jackets and yellow breeches broke into the clearing, announcing themselves as an advance guard of Lee's Legion, sent to rejoin Marion by the orders of General Greene.

Light Horse Harry Lee himself, the grinning newcomers reported, was only a few days behind them, with the main body of his Legion. And General Greene was also at that moment riding southward to reopen the fight for South Carolina.

Marion was the only one who remained silent in the explosive moment that followed the startling announcement. Every other member of the Brigade was hoarsely cheering the new arrivals, and the new hope that had sprung alive there in the clearing with their sudden appearance out of the forest into the circle of firelight.

CHAPTER

XIII

That same night Marion learned from the officer in command of Lee's advance detachment exactly what had been happening to Greene's Southern Army since its escape into Virginia and, even more importantly, what Greene's plans were for the future.

Greene, Marion discovered, had never abandoned his original intention of fighting Cornwallis. After his men had recuperated from their wild dash northward, with the British at their heels, Greene had rested and reorganized his force while Lee's Legion had gone back into North Carolina to harass Cornwallis' recruiting efforts with partisan tactics. Then Greene had marched south again as far as Guilford Courthouse in North Carolina. There, on March 15, 1781, he and Cornwallis finally met in a bloody battle. Greene left the field first and Cornwallis claimed the victory. But the British loss had been so heavy that day—one third of Cornwallis' army had been either killed or wounded—that when news of the battle reached England a member of Parliament remarked acidly, "Another such victory would destroy the British Army."

Greene was aware of how seriously he had mauled the enemy and would have liked nothing better than a chance to offer the British a second victory of the same sort. But Cornwallis had hastily moved east to await reinforcements at the port of Wilmington, North Carolina. Greene therefore started south again, intending to strike next in the state where Marion and Sumter had been holding out almost alone for many weeks. He hoped to destroy the two major inland garrisons England still had there even after Cornwallis' abandonment of Winnsboro. These two posts, Ninety-Six and Camden, were both under the command of Cornwallis' deputy, the youthful Lord Francis Rawdon. Rawdon's main force at Camden was actually no larger than Greene's own. And the Quaker Patriot believed that if the Carolina partisans harried Rawdon's supply lines and prevented him from receiving reinforcements, the American Southern Army would be able to meet the recoats on more than equal terms.

Marion needed no more explicit orders. He dispatched couriers to collect his recently disbanded men as quickly as possible. He sent out scouts to lead Lee and his Legion—and the supplies Marion assumed they had—to his own temporary encampment. He began to collect fresh intelligence about the enemy against which he had been helpless only the day before, but which he now planned to attack as soon as Lee arrived.

The first vital news Marion received was about Watson. That British officer, who had left Georgetown with nine hundred men to hunt for the Swamp Fox, had changed his mind abruptly when he learned that his quarry was about to receive Continental reinforcements. Watson had dumped his two cannon into Catfish Creek, burned the bulk of his supplies in a huge bonfire and started back toward Georgetown at top speed.

Marion was tempted by the prospect of chasing Watson once more, but he recognized the impracticality of the plan as soon as Lee arrived. The Legion had as little ammunition as Marion himself. Greene had been so scantily supplied that he had been unable to furnish Lee with either bullets or powder, and none had been available on the way south. So Marion and Lee agreed to move instead on Fort Watson, near Nelson's Ferry, in the hope of seizing the considerable store of ammuition the British were known to keep there.

Marion and Lee had failed to assault the fort on the previous occasion when they had been together because their rifles and muskets had been no match for the artillery mounted on the fort's walls—the very guns Watson had now destroyed. The fort still presented a considerable problem, however. It stood on an old Indian mound raised some thirty feet above the surrounding flat country, and if the Patriots tried to approach it closely they would come within range of the defenders' musket fire. But the garrison's water was obtained from a small lake outside the walls, and Marion hoped the fort could be forced to surrender if access to that lake was cut off.

As usual Marion and Lee moved fast once their minds were made up. By the early evening of April 15, the very day after Lee had joined Marion, their combined force formed a circle of carefully spaced men around the foot of the mound on which the stockade stood. Fire from within the walls soon forced them to move back out of range, but the circle remained intact.

The fort's commander, Lieutenant James McKay, proved more resourceful than many British officers Marion had encountered. He withdrew most of his men from the walls, and set them to work in relays digging a well. The excavation had to go down a long way—through the mound—in order to reach water in the earth below. But ceaseless work accomplished the labor within a surprisingly short time. Soon the British were calling tauntingly from the walls that they had struck water inside the fort. The fort's defenders and attackers were at a stalemate. The British could not injure the Americans provided they kept their distance. The Americans could not take a fort that they dared not approach.

Marion, in the meantime, had sent an urgent request to Greene for a cannon that could batter down the log walls. But he knew the request could not be filled for many days, at best, and that time was on the British side. It was always possible that McKay had already sent for help. And if a new British force arrived from Georgetown, Charleston or any other garrison, well supplied with ammunition, Marion and Lee would have to run.

On the seventh tense day of waiting, in the warm spring sunshine around Fort Watson, one of Marion's officers had an ingenious idea. He suggested that a log tower, built high enough to rise above the fort's walls, would enable American sharpshooters to expend their few bullets in deadly shots straight down into the interior of the fort. Marion, instantly appreciating the value of the plan, sent some of his men out to borrow a supply of axes from farms in the neighborhood. That night Legionaires and members of the Brigade were busily felling and trimming trees and carrying the logs up the mound to within rifle range of the walls. Other men piled the logs, crisscross fashion, into a flimsy structure that was twice as high as the fort's walls. By dawn a handful of Marion's best riflemen had climbed to the top of the shaky tower and huddled down behind the top layer of logs. When the British began to stir in the early light of day they were staggered to hear the deadly whine of bullets around their ears. Only then did they see the tower that reared up less than a hundred yards away.

The effect was instantaneous. The American fire was so accurate that the entire besieged garrison had to cower at the foot of the wall nearest the tower, the only place invisible to the elevated marksmen. Marion and Lee took quick advantage of the enemy's immobility. They sent a party of men around the fort to start prying away the logs of the wall on the far side. If the British attempted to move across the interior of the fort to put a stop to this activity, they would be exposing themselves to fire from the tower. Even their newly dug well was effectively out of reach of the British.

Lieutenant McKay proved he was intelligent as well as resourceful. Aware that prolonging the siege would mean only a senseless loss of life, he sent out a flag of truce and the offer to surrender his garrison of forty Tories and twice as many British regulars. The siege had cost the Patriots eight days. It had won for them the valuable arms and ammunition the fort storehouse held. It also introduced into Patriot warfare the so-called Maham tower, named after its inventor, Colonel Hezekiah Maham.

In the letter that Marion sent off by courier to Greene right after the British surrender, he commended Maham's scheme and added with characteristic generosity, "In short, sir, I have had the greatest assistance from everyone under my command." He added that he would, "without loss of time, proceed to demolish the fort; after which I shall march to the high hills of the Santee, encamp at Capt. Richardson's, and await your orders."

The hills of the Santee—the High Hills of Santee, as they were usually called—were an irregular chain of sand hills approximately two hundred feet high and twenty-four miles long, located just east of the Wateree River and overlooking the road that led to Camden some twenty miles to the north. Marion's purpose in posting himself and Lee's Legion there was to prevent Watson from using that road to join the British army in Camden, which Greene hoped soon to entice out into the open where he could attack it with better prospects of success.

Lord Rawdon, at Camden, was immediately alerted to the presence of the Swamp Fox at his rear. He decided that Marion was either on his way to reinforce Greene or planning a two-pronged attack on Camden in conjunction with Greene. The British commander didn't like either possibility. In a quick and sudden move he sent his full force out of camp and attacked Greene's encampment on Hobkirk's Hill, a short distance from Camden.

The Patriots weren't prepared for this abrupt onslaught. They were washing or mending clothes and eating breakfast when the pickets began to fire at the advancing British. Greene managed to get his lines in order before Rawdon's main attack, but was eventually driven back several miles, leaving Rawdon in possession of Hobkirk's Hill. The British, however, had suffered some serious losses, and instead of pursuing the Americans, they retreated back to their fortified position at Camden to await Watson and his reinforcing regiments.

Greene now called on Lee's Legion for help, and Marion was left on the Santee Hills with only a small force—too small a force to watch over that large area. In consequence, Watson was able to make a large circle westward and move north to

Camden on the west side of the Wateree River, keeping that stream between himself and Marion's depleted body of men. On May 7 he arrived at Camden with five hundred men. Rawdon immediately moved out from there, this time bent on Greene's total destruction. Greene saved his army from an annihilating attack only by moving back to a position so well protected by natural defenses that not even Rawdon's superior force dared assault it. But once sheltered in that position Greene dared not leave it. Thus once again any active warfare that took place in South Carolina would necessarily have to be carried out by the partisans.

Marion's partisans, however, had not been returning as rapidly as he had anticipated. He might have stimulated enlistments if, like Sumter, he offered to pay recruits with slaves captured from Tory plantations, at the rate of one grown Negro to every private, and three grown Negroes and one Negro boy to every colonel. But Marion could not approve of this arrangement. His objection was in no way an objection to slavery itself, then a fully accepted institution in the colonies. He simply believed that looted property of any kind—that is, property obtained by what he regarded as organized robbery—should not be offered as payment for military service. He further felt that men recruited by such a system would themselves be more enthusiastic looters than fighters. So he preferred to see his own command shrunk almost to nothing rather than swell the Brigade by promises of stolen wealth.

Marion's followers, however, slowly proved that their commander's faith in them was justified. They began to drift back to the Santee Hills as their spring chores were completed. When Watson scurried around the partisans on his dash to Camden, Marion had only a hundred or so men. By the time the Englishman reached Camden the Brigade was twice as strong. When Greene decided to retreat to his impregnable position north of Camden, and once more sent Lee southward to join Marion, the Swamp Fox believed himself powerful enough to make an attempt on Fort Motte.

The British had not actually built Fort Motte. They had simply taken over a large new hilltop mansion—evicted the owner, Mrs. Rebecca Motte, to a servant's cabin and surrounded the mansion with a tall, heavy, log stockade. A deep ditch around the outside of the wall provided further protection to the fort's defenders, and firing apertures gave their muskets complete coverage of the hill on which the mansion stood.

Mrs. Motte welcomed Lee and Marion into her small cramped house when they arrived in the neighborhood early in May. Lee made the cottage his headquarters, while Marion and his men pitched camp on the side of the hill below the fort and beyond range of its muskets. There too Marion set up the single six-pound cannon with which Greene had recently provided him, and prepared to batter down the fort's walls.

First, of course, he sent the usual demand for surrender to Fort Motte's commander, a Lieutenant McPherson, and—also as usual—McPherson refused. The British officer was well supplied with food, water and ammunition for his one hundred fifty men, and confident that Rawdon would reinforce him before his walls could be breached by any means the Patriots had at their command.

Marion, watching his first few cannon balls bounce harmlessly off the log walls, was inclined to subscribe to McPherson's own view of impregnability. The British walls were clearly too strong for his six-pound shot. They would obviously yield only to charges of gunpowder, or to the forceful blows of an ax. Either form of attack would require the Americans to climb the open and exposed slope of the hill, where they would meet certain death from the British muskets.

Marion and Lee discussed their dilemma. They discarded the use of a Maham tower as being impossible in this particular situation, and finally reached the only conclusion that seemed feasible. They set their men to digging approach trenches that would zigzag their way to the very foot of the walls, and thus give the Americans a protected means of attacking the logs.

The work began in four-hour shifts, and proceeded so rapidly that at the end of a single day Marion believed McPherson must now recognize the hopelessness of his situation. But McPherson refused a second surrender demand as calmly as he had refused the first. His duty, as he saw it, he said, was to resist to the last extremity.

That same night, however, a courier from Greene reined in his lathered horse at Marion's tent and handed the Brigade commander a dispatch. It said that Rawdon had abandoned Camden—because his supply lines to that place had been so seriously disrupted by partisan attacks—and was moving toward Fort Motte with his entire army. Marion and Lee both knew they couldn't withstand an attack by Rawdon. They realized that if they were to capture the fort they would have to do it before he arrived. So the work on the trenches began again under cover of darkness, and went on at a feverish pace all the following morning. By noon the trenches had been extended so close to the walls that the diggers were in constant danger from carefully aimed muskets inside the stockade, and necessary caution slowed down their progress. But still they kept on.

During the afternoon scouts brought in the news that Rawdon was rapidly approaching on the far side of the river. That night, as Legionaires and members of the Brigade went on working in the trenches, they could see the many fires of Rawdon's encampment at a distance of only a few miles. But the Americans knew that Rawdon would have to march his army all the way down to Nelson's Ferry before he could cross the river, so they went on with their digging.

By the next morning it was clear that the trenches would be completed by noon. But if the Americans had seen Rawdon's fires in the night, McPherson had undoubtedly seen them too. Marion suspected that the British officer, knowing help to be close at hand, would be prepared to fight a bloody battle, even if his walls were breached. McPherson might even manage to hold out until Rawdon sent a fast cavalry detachment to relieve him. Reluctantly Marion and Lee decided that their best chance of success lay in burning the enemy out immediately. Destroying Mrs. Motte's house was a step they hated to take. But she herself did more than merely agree to it. She offered the two commanders a bow and several incendiary arrows, with the suggestion that they might be used to start the conflagration of her own home.

Legend says the bow and arrows were actually used for that purpose. Historians disagree on the point. But there is no doubt that at noon, on May 11, either by an incendiary arrow, or by some other means, the roof of the mansion was set afire. McPherson had been given a final chance to surrender and for the third time had refused. Within minutes after the receipt of his answer the roof's dry shingles were ablaze and smoke was rising from the house in a tall black column.

McPherson put up a gallant defense. He ordered a party of his men into the attic of the house, to rip loose the burning shingles and hurl them to the ground. But the instant the first gaping hole appeared in the roof, Marion signaled the artillerymen stationed beside his six-pounder.

The little cannon boomed once, and a charge of grapeshot zoomed over the log walls to slice through that opening.

Immediately afterward a white flag was thrust out from the fort. Marion accepted the offer of surrender the moment it was made, and sent his own men into the fort to help deal with the flames. Most of the house was saved from serious damage.

That night, once they had assured themselves that Rawdon was still a safe distance away, Marion and Lee accepted Mrs. Motte's invitation to the celebration dinner she had hastily prepared. Generously she invited the officers of the defeated British post too, and briefly across her table McPherson and his conquerors shared the thoughts and words of civilized men who might, under other circumstances, have become friends.

Only one unfortunate incident marred the occasion and reminded every man present that the brutality of war could never be forgotten as long as the war itself continued. Marion, called from the table by the whispered words of one of his men, found that an unruly crowd of Lee's Legionaires had hanged three

Tory prisoners on a crudely constructed gallows, as part of their own victory celebration. Marion beat his way into the center of the mob with the flat of his sword, cut down the victims—only one of them was still alive—and then turned the cold fire of his anger on the soldiers who had chosen to mark their own triumph with the cruel death of three helpless enemies. In a voice few had ever heard him use before, he threatened to kill with his own hands the next man who molested a prisoner of war.

The men fell back and dispersed. Within a few minutes Marion stood alone. But the sword he so seldom used was still in his hands, his face was still dark with rage at the inhumanity of men to their fellow men.

Lee, when he learned what had happened, was probably as shocked as Marion had been. In almost every military experience which they had met together, the Virginia-born regular soldier and the South Carolina partisan had thought basically alike even if they sometimes disagreed on tactics. Only on a single occasion did Lee's apparent misunderstanding of Marion's role in the war bring about trouble. But it was trouble so critical that it prompted Marion to offer Greene his resignation.

The unfortunate situation began when Lee wrote a letter to Greene in which he said, "General Marion can supply you, if he will, with 150 good dragoon horses . . ." Lee certainly understood that Marion's men needed horses in order to carry out the swift raids which made them the terror of the British. But perhaps he thought Greene's cavalry could make even better use of the mounts. Or perhaps he honestly believed, at the time he wrote that letter, that Marion had horses to spare beyond those he actually used day by day.

When Greene received the letter, however, he seems to have read into it only one meaning: that Marion possessed horses he did not need, but which he selfishly refused to contribute to Greene's always underequipped cavalry. Greene wrote immediately to Marion, reproaching him for not having sent him horses when, according to Lee, he could easily have done so.

Marion had never asked anything for himself since he became a partisan leader. He had asked nothing for his Brigade except, occasionally, ammunition to be expended in the Patriot cause. He was hurt to think that Greene considered him capable of withholding any contribution it was within his power to make for that cause. He thought Greene should have known that if he had horses he didn't need he would have sent them to Greene. If, on the other hand, Greene expected him to give up the horses his own men were using, this suggested that Greene did not, after all, believe the partisans' work to be important—that he was willing to see it abandoned if it would provide more horses for the Continental Army. But whatever Greene thought, his letter seemed to imply either that the partisan leader was a selfish officer unfit for his command, or that his entire Brigade could be disepnsed with. Marion's reply to Greene expressed his sense of injury and closed with a request for permission to resign.

Greene was a much harassed man, who sometimes—and understandably—let his temper run away with him. But Marion's letter apparently shocked him into the realization that his own hasty and ill-considered words might cost him, and the cause he shared with Marion, the services of an unusual leader and all the men who followed him. He hastily wrote another and frankly apologetic letter to Marion in which he said:

> My reasons for writing so pressingly respecting the dragoons was from the distress we were in. It is not my wish to take horses from the militia ... You have rendered important service ... and done great honor to yourself; and I would not wish to render your situation less agreeable ...

That letter ended the controversy as far as Marion was concerned. He spoke no more about his resignation, and at the first opportunity sent Greene a fine horse for his own use, as proof that he bore no grudge. But the controversy had done at least temporary harm to the Brigade. Many of its members, convinced that they were about to be dismounted, were drifting away. By the time Lee and his Legion left Marion in order to join Sumter temporarily, on the day after Fort Motte surrendered, the Brigade had shrunk alarmingly. Marion had less than a hundred and fifty men with him when he moved south shortly afterward to keep a watchful eye on Rawdon's encampment at Nelson's Ferry, and to follow Rawdon when he cautiously withdrew to Monck's Corner, thirty miles closer to the protection of Charleston. Marion's chief purpose was to prevent Rawdon from dashing inland again to relieve Ninety-Six, to which Greene was then laying siege.

But the slow passage of days brought Marion new recruits, inspired by the recent Patriot successes. He was able to dispatch Horry with a sizable party into the Williamsburg district in response to appeals for help from there. The Tory Major Gainey, in the saddle again after recuperating from the bayonet wound Sergeant McDonald had inflicted on him, was once more raiding plantations along the Pee Dee. Gainey proved unwilling to risk a battle with the partisans, and eventually signed a treaty with Horry that brought an uneasy peace to Williamsburg. By the time that treaty was signed on June 17 another event had occurred even more gratifying to the South Carolina Patriots.

Marion had learned that the garrison at Georgetown had been reduced and, leaving Maham behind to watch Rawdon, he started off on a forced march to make one more attempt on that previously unassailable British stronghold. One June 5 he came up before the town's fortifications and prepared to besiege them.

Georgetown's commander made the siege unnecessary. That same night he loaded all his men and as many supplies as he could carry on board boats, and sailed for Charleston.

Marion marched unchallenged into the deserted town the next day. He took over the remaining supplies, razed the fortifications, and—for the first time in many long months—quartered himself in a house and experienced the unusual luxury of four solid walls and a bed. He even acquired some new uniforms. And, because his ever-present Oscar had appropriated a bag of coffee beans from the British warehouse, Marion was able to drink something other than vinegar and water at his first breakfast in the new headquarters.

Tree-shaded little Georgetown, surrounded by the swamps he had known in his boyhood, was full of memories for him. His father had tilled some of the fields that brought the town its first wealth in terms of rice. His Brigade had had its birth there, on the day the British Captain Ardesoif had arrogantly threatened Major James and sent him home to Williamsburg to rouse his neighbors to rebellion. Twice Marion himself had tried to break the enemy's hold on the strategic port, and twice he had failed. Now Georgetown was a Patriot stronghold and Marion was its honored liberator.

But the satisfaction he must have felt there was abruptly shattered by what at first appeared to be a major catastrophe for the Patriot cause. Only a few days after Marion entered Georgetown, a British fleet reached Charleston with three Irish regiments aboard. As soon as they disembarked they marched straight inland to Monck's Corner to join Rawdon, and Rawdon thereupon set off for Ninety-Six with a force of two thousand men.

Marion's Brigade, even at its fullest strength, could not have stopped Rawdon's newly swollen army. Under the circumstances, with Horry still in Williamsburg and the rest of the Brigade divided between Georgetown and Monck's Corner, Marion was helpless. All he could do was send the grim news to Sumter who forwarded it to Greene. And all Greene could do was to call off the exhausting siege he had been conducting for a full month. On June 19 he broke up his encampment outside the stout walls of Ninety-Six and hurried his men out of Rawdon's reach.

Ninety-Six was the last of the three major British fortifications that had once formed a semicircle through the Up Country some hundred and fifty miles inland from the Carolina coast. Winnsboro had been abandoned when Cornwallis took off after Greene; with Cornwallis now being harried eastward through Virginia by a Patriot force under Lafayette, it was unlikely that

Winnsboro would again be occupied by the British. Camden, too, had been abandoned.

During the past few months the Patriots had shattered every British line of communication within the northern and northwestern parts of the area by destroying most of the posts the British had set up to guard those routes. On April 13 Colonel William Harden, one of Marion's officers, had captured Fort Balfour at Pocotaligo, on the road inland from Beaufort and only thirty miles from that British coastal stronghold. A week later Marion and Lee had taken and destroyed Fort Watson. On the single day of May 11 Fort Motte had fallen to Marion and Lee, and the fort at Orangeburg had fallen to Sumter. Four days afterward Sumter, freshly reinforced by Lee, had taken the British garrison at Granby. Even Augusta, Georgia, had yielded to a besieging force led by Lee and the Carolina partisan Andrew Pickens. Now Marion also held Georgetown, one of the three coastal bases from which the British supply trains normally set out.

Under these circumstances Rawdon was too good a strategist to attempt to hold Ninety-Six. Shortly after Greene's flight from the immediate neighborhood he evacuated the fort, and led his troops back toward Charleston, trailed by a long line of Tory sympathizers afraid to remain behind in the now thoroughly Patriot Up Country.

One more officially British victory had proved itself to be far less of a victory than it appeared on the surface.

Rawdon decided that he would be unable to hold any British establishment more than seventy miles from the coast, from Charleston itself, and decided upon Orangeburg as the site of this one deep inland garrison. The place had been practically deserted since Sumter defeated the British encamped there, and the fort had to be completely rebuilt after that assault. So Rawdon stopped off at Orangeburg on his way to the coast, having already ordered Colonel Alexander Stewart (sometimes spelled Stuart) to march out of Charleston with four hundred men and building equipment and meet him there.

Reassessing their activities of the past few weeks, the Patriots were beginning to realize the extent of their triumphs. Hopefully they made plans for the future.

The combined forces of Rawdon and Stewart were too strong to be attacked, but Sumter suggested that their camp at Orangeburg might be cut off from Charleston by assaults against all the smaller British posts between that city and the newly built Orangeburg fort. Greene, whose men were enjoying a period of much-needed rest, though watching Rawdon and Stewart at the same time, agreed to the plan. He put Sumter in command of the operation, at the head of an army of nearly a thousand men, consisting of Sumter's own partisans, Lee's Legion, and Marion's Brigade of unpaid volunteers.

Sumter chose as his primary objective a sizable British body at Monck's Corner commanded by a Lieutenant Colonel Coates. While he prepared that move he assigned part of his army, under Lee and Colonel Wade Hampton, to a series of diversionary raids close to Charleston. The raids were so successful that the city was soon in an uproar, much as it had been long before when the British first threatened to seize it. The streets were full of soldiers hastening to man the defenses, and houses shook with the booming of alarm guns.

But Sumter's own plans for Monck's Corner were less fully carried out. Coates, warned of his approach, had moved all his supplies across Wadboo Creek to Biggin Church, fortified that strong brick building and waited behind its walls for Sumter's attack.

The Brigade's responsibility was the destruction of the bridge over Wadboo Creek, on the enemy's major road of retreat back to Charleston. Maham and Horry, assigned to the job, routed the first party of British sent out against them. But they had still not completely demolished the bridge when a second British party arrived, stronger than the first, and the Americans were forced to retreat under its assault.

There had been good reason for Tarleton bestowing the nickname of Gamecock on Sumter. Sumter fought as bravely as any gamecock, but sometimes he showed no more than a gamecock's judgment. Now, mistakenly believing that the British party from which Horry and Maham had fled was actually Coates' main force, Sumter prepared to meet it from a strong position in a ravine. He was waiting there, ready to strike at the first sight of the enemy, while Coates hastily set fire to Biggin Church and his stores there, and led his men across the still passable Wadboo Bridge in a quick retreat toward Quinby Bridge, ten miles to the south on the road to Charleston.

Not until three o'clock in the morning, when flames burst through the church roof, did Sumter realize that he had been outwitted. He immediately ordered his full force to take off after Coates, cavalry in the lead, infantrymen following at their best possible speed.

The British were safely across Quinby Bridge, and were destroying it behind them, before the American cavalry caught up with their quarry. Fearlessly the Patriots dashed across the loosened planks of the span, leaping the gaps where the timbers had already been ripped out, to engage the British rear guard on the narrow causeway beyond the bridge. Coates was in personal command of a small group of officers and men who staved off the Patriots' sabers with brilliant swordplay, while the main body of British troops rallied to their aid. The British reinforcements were about to charge when the Americans realized that the bridge behind them had collapsed into the stream. Swiftly and valorously they plunged straight through the British and escaped by riding furiously upstream along the forested bank.

Coates showed his respect for the American cavalry by a move calculated to avoid another engagement. He occupied a plantation nearby, so well surrounded by outbuildings and fences that a mounted attack would be impossible.

At three o'clock the following afternoon Sumter, having been forced to make a wide detour to bypass the destroyed bridge, brought his full force up to within sight of the plantation. Characteristically he decided upon an immediate assault, despite the fact that he had failed to bring with him artillery for battering down the walls of the plantation house and thus forcing the enemy out into the open. Marion advised him to send for cannon and delay action until the guns arrived. But caution was not one of Sumter's strong points. He disliked Marion's suggestion and, being in command, was in a position to ignore it. So it was Sumter's plan that was adopted and it was Sumter who arranged the placement of the various forces under his command. His own companies were given a position behind a line of small outbuildings used as slave quarters. Marion's two companies were ordered to the right of the house, where their only shelter was a rail fence.

At four o'clock Sumter gave the command to advance, and the British opened a hot fire from the protection of the house. One of Sumter's companies, moving bravely past the outbuildings, was met by a sharp British bayonet attack and fell back hastily. Marion's men rushed to the rescue, drove the British back into the house and enabled Sumter's soldiers to regain their own shelters. Then the members of the Brigade clung to their advance post and continued to fire at every target that presented itself. Only when their ammunition was entirely exhausted did they retreat, taking their numerous dead and wounded with them.

Sumter called off the attack at sundown, determined to reopen it again the following day. But three hours of bloody and useless fighting had cost him heavy losses and the confidence of even his own men. Many of them disappeared during the night, along with many more of Marion's, who felt they had been given the most dangerous positions in the battle. Lee left with his Legion in the morning. At the same time news reached Sumter that Rawdon was moving toward Quinby Bridge, and that further reinforcements might be coming from Charleston to help Coates. Sumter then saw the foolishness of a second attempt, and he departed northward to a position not far from where Greene was resting his army. Marion and what was left of his Brigade moved to a post from which they could keep an eye on the lower Santee.

It was mid-July. The main British and American forces were both half-sick and almost totally exhausted from the intense heat of the Southern summer. Protected from each other by the Congaree and Wateree rivers, and the swamps along both streams, neither side was eager to seek action. Both were content to watch each other until the cooling breezes of autumn had revived their strength.

CHAPTER XIV

South Carolina was not the only inactive theater during that seventh summer of the war. New England, too, had seen no serious fighting for a long time. Sir Henry Clinton still quietly occupied New York. General Washington, unable to obtain the aid of a French fleet for a joint attack on that city, still camped on the hills above the Hudson and awaited an opportunity for some decisive action.

But suddenly, late in August, Washington gave up his long-held dream of retaking New York and headed south with his entire army of seven thousand French and American soldiers, supply wagons and artillery—a long snakelike column that moved slowly through the heat under a blazing sky. The marching feet and the clomping hoofs of the horses kicked up a pall of dust that could be seen for miles. Washington's original destination was Charleston, and his original purpose the seizure of that palmetto-shaded city which the British had now held for over a year. A dispatch from Lafayette, informing him that Cornwallis had moved into the Yorktown peninsula of Virginia, had caused him to change his plan. Unless the British general received reinforcements by sea, he was cut off from all help in that cul-de-sac and peculiarly vulnerable to attack. Washington knew that Admiral de Grasse, commander of a French fleet in the West Indies, was willing to come as far north as Virginia, even though he had refused to come to New York. So Washington decided to combine with de Grasse and Lafayette in a land-and-sea assault designed to close the trap into which Cornwallis had walked.

Washington's move revived activity in South Carolina. Greene's army, still worn out and needing both supplies and reinforcements, nevertheless broke camp immediately and moved closer to the British, in order to occupy their attention at once if they showed signs of going to Cornwallis' aid.

Marion knew he might be called to join Greene at any moment, and was prepared to do so. But before he received orders to that effect, a courier brought him a letter begging his help for Colonel Harden, who had formerly served with the Brigade but was now leading his own group of Patriot volunteers.

Harden's situation was serious. As one of the few partisan officers who had remained almost constantly active during the summer's terrible heat, raiding under the very noses of the British along the Edisto River just southeast of Charleston, he had invited severe retaliation. A party of several hundred Tories, far superior to his own command in numbers and equipment, had been sent out from Charleston under the command of a Major C. Fraser, with the express purpose of destroying his force. With his weary band Harden had been hiding and running and hiding again from Fraser's Tories. The letter he sent to Marion said he could not hold out much longer unless he received help.

Marion obtained official approval from Greene and set off quickly to Harden's aid with two hundred picked men. At the same time he sent a small party of mounted partisans to raid near Monck's Corner and Dorchester, so that British forces at those places would not be moved out to reinforce Harden's enemy. The hundred-mile journey to the Edisto River from Marion's camp led across two main lines of communications, so Marion had to travel at night. But he slipped past British patrols in safety and joined a much-relieved Harden on the last day of August.

The plan of action Marion devised was aimed at Fraser's

cavalry, the most dangerous unit in the Tory officer's command. Because he felt sure Fraser was completely unaware of his arrival in the neighborhood, and in any case was unfamiliar with his methods, Marion decided to employ his old decoy stratagem. But this time a small group of cavalrymen played the role of decoy, rather than Marion himself.

The trick worked superbly. Having hidden most of his men close to the enemy camp, in a causeway-traversed swamp near Parker's Ferry, Marion sent the decoy party out. They rode straight toward Fraser's tents, but as if unaware of the Tories' proximity until they saw evidence that they had been sighted by Fraser's guards. Then, in apparently sudden alarm, they turned and galloped away toward the causeway alongside of which the rest of the Brigade members were concealed.

Fraser thought he had at last flushed Harden out into the open. Triumphantly he led his own cavalry out in pursuit of the fleeing partisans. The Tories were pounding along the causeway, heedless of anything but the nearness of their quarry, when the underbrush beside them exploded noisily with the fire of nearly two hundred guns.

Through mushrooming billows of heavy acrid smoke Fraser shouted to his men, some of whom were already dead or seriously wounded, while the rest were trying to free themselves from dead mounts' stirrups or to control unharmed but frantically rearing beasts. The British officer ordered his company to turn off the road and charge into the swamp at the unseen enemy. At least a part of his disorganized cavalrymen attempted to obey, but a second volley thundering out of the underbrush threw them once more into turmoil. More horses collapsed. More lifeless bodies tumbled from saddles to be dragged through the dust and trampled under crashing hooves.

Fraser had had enough. He ordered immediate retreat. But as the survivors among his men freed themselves to race back down the way they had come, they passed through a third volley of mutilating buckshot and deadly rifle balls. Even the sight of their infantry, running toward them down the causeway to join in the fray, didn't halt their terrified dash toward the safety of the camp.

The powder horns of Marion's men were nearly empty. The partisans would be no match for the numerous and well-armed foe now approaching down the road. Marion ordered an instant withdrawal and led his men back into the concealing swamp so swiftly that Fraser's fresh troops could find no trace of them.

Harden had been rescued. He would later perform notable service as the commander of a company with Pickens' Brigade. Marion made his way back to his camp on the Santee in time to receive General Greene's letter of September 4, ordering him to join the Continental Army then advancing on the main British force.

Lord Rawdon having retired because of illness, General Stewart was now in sole command of that force. When scouts reported that Greene was advancing toward him, Stewart quickly retreated from his Orangeburg camp to a little settlement called Eutaw Springs, not more than forty miles from Charleston. Stewart didn't know where Marion was at the time, but he did know he wasn't with Greene. And since he felt sure Greene wouldn't launch an attack without the help of the Swamp Fox and his two hundred men, Stewart rested easily at his new camp. What he didn't know, of course, having had little experience in Carolina, was how swiftly Marion could move when he wished. Actually Marion was circling around him, even as Stewart idly wondered where he might be, and had reached a place only seventeen miles above the British encampment.

Greene joined Marion there almost immediately, and together they started a southward march toward the enemy. Still Stewart didn't suspect their presence in the neighborhood. When two deserters from Greene's force told him, early on the morning of September 8, that Greene was only a few miles away, Stewart simply didn't believe them. But minutes later a few survivors of one of his own scouting parties came in, with the news that Greene's men had killed the rest of their group—and that Greene and his whole Patriot force were within four miles of the British camp and moving steadily forward. In a frenzy of belated activity, then, Stewart sent out skirmishing parties and ordered the bulk of his men to leave their half-finished breakfasts and prepare for immediate attack.

Greene placed the partisans in the front of his advancing battle line that day. Marion and his men were on the right. Sumter's men were on the left. Between them strode a party of North Carolina volunteers under Colonel Francis Malmedy. And, perhaps because he trusted regular troops more than he did volunteers, Greene backed up the front line with his Continentals from Virginia, Maryland and North Carolina.

But Greene could find no fault with the way the partisans advanced. Straight through Stewart's skirmishers they moved, with the coolness of the best regular troops, and on to Stewart's hastily drawn-up lines. They were firing steadily, and as rapidly as their slow-loading muskets and rifles permitted. Under a heavy rain of British bullets they marched on without stopping until they had driven the British back for half a mile.

Only then, when their ammunition ran out, did they begin to falter. Marion, seeing a British bayonet charge in the making, ordered the bayonetless partisans to fall back. Greene brought the Continentals up to take their place, fixed bayonets at the ready to meet the enemy's flashing steel. Then the Continentals in their turn engaged the British, forcing them back still farther and throwing them into complete disorder.

The British withdrawal appeared to be reducing itself to a rout. Yard after yard Stewart's men gave way, retreating hastily through their own camping area and into the woods beyond it. Jubilantly the Americans drove after them until they were among the deserted British tents.

There the sight of the enemy's abandoned breakfast accomplished what Stewart's guns and sabers had been unable to do. It stopped the advancing Patriots in their tracks. Greedily the hungry men grabbed up half-cooked or half-consumed food and wolfed it down. Thirstily they emptied every canteen of rum they saw. Within a few brief and amazing moments the

American front lines had completely disintegrated. Organized companies had become disorganized knots of men so busy eating and drinking at the redcoats' expense that they had forgotten to fight the redcoats themselves.

Stewart made quick use of the surprising advantage thus thrust into his hands. From the security of a sturdy brick house not far away, his riflemen directed a burst of fire at the Continentals who had dropped their weapons to snatch pieces of roasted meat or to quarrel over the last drops of liquor in a jug. Patriot officers who were trying frantically to recall their men to duty were among the dozens felled by enemy bullets. While the catastrophic riot continued Steward organized counterattacks that closed in on the tenting area from both sides.

Greene, almost speechless with rage, issued the order for a retreat. Pausing only long enough to pick up his wounded, he led his demoralized army back along the route it had so recently and so gallantly traveled, led it back in disgrace from the field it had so nearly won. The only accomplishment the Patriots could claim that day was that they had left Stewart's army too heavily buffeted to be able to follow up their retreat. Stewart, in fact, although he held the field of battle for the rest of that day, had suffered so many losses that he gave up his Eutaw Springs camp the next morning. Having burned his stores —though he did not take time to bury all of his dead, or even to care for all of his wounded—he moved coastward as far as Monck's Corner. He claimed the victory, of course. Greene claimed it too, once Stewart had fled.

Marion's Brigade, which had seen furious action in the courageous advance on Eutaw Springs, started off after the British as soon as they began to retreat. But the partisans failed to catch Stewart before he was joined by a strong body of reinforcements at Monck's Corner, and were not numerous enough to attack the freshly strengthened British force there. Marion then followed Greene's example and led his men across the Santee where his wounded could recover and his scouts could keep an eye on any significant move the British might make.

Within a comparatively short time the Patriots had pushed the British out of the entire state of South Carolina, except for a semicircular area arcing inland from Charleston for a distance of not more than fifty miles. Yet the military situation of the partisans was at the moment extremely precarious. Greene had less than a thousand men fit for duty. The various partisan groups were all very small. Neither Continentals nor partisans had enough ammunition for even a day-long engagement.

Their enemy's situation, on the other hand, was very different. The British were certainly alarmed at the trap that had begun to spring shut around Cornwallis as Washington and the French fleet closed in on the Yorktown peninsula at the end of September. They must have realized that Cornwallis was as good as lost, and that after his defeat the French fleet and the entire American army might come south to attack their stronghold at Charleston. Certainly they were consciously preparing to withstand a siege of that city or to evacuate it in favor of Savannah. But they were in excellent condition to pursue either of these two courses.

Having been forced to pull back their outposts, they had a lot of manpower in a relatively small area. They had two thousand troops stationed at Nelson's Ferry and three hundred more at Monck's Corner, while the Charleston garrison was swollen by Tories who had retreated coastward with the British rather than face vengeful Patriots in their own neighborhoods. Ships continued to arrive in Charleston from England, laden with munitions, and with uniforms and medicines sufficient for all the redcoats under arms and for any new Tory regiments that might yet be formed.

The British force's only serious lacks were fodder for their horses and enough food for the concentrated mass in and around Charleston. Consequently their major activity, throughout the still-hot weeks of the early fall, was to raid the countryside for those items—and for any slaves, silver or other forms of Carolina wealth they might seize while there was still time. Official British foraging parties scoured the entire territory between the Santee and the Edisto rivers, and groups of Tory partisans successfully duplicated the tactics so brilliantly evolved by Marion and Sumter. Even the Tory Gainey, theoretically bound by the truce Horry had forced him to sign, began to stir again along the Pee Dee.

It was a tribute to Marion's reputation that none of the raiding or foraging parties dared to cross the Santee when they learned he was encamped on its far side. Had they realized how few bullets Marion's men carried in their pouches, they would scarcely have been so cautious. But they didn't know, and consequently regarded the whole area north of the Santee as out of bounds to even the most fearless looters.

It was no doubt gratifying to Marion to realize that he could protect a sizable portion of Carolina by his mere presence. But he was chafing at the inactivity enforced on his men by lack of ammunition. Early in October he wrote to Greene and to the exiled President Rutledge, asking them both for powder and lead. Rutledge's reply said, "I wish to God it was in my power to send you ammunition instantly, but it is not." From General Greene's camp came the answer, "Our stock of ammunition is quite exhausted—we have not an ounce of powder, or a cartridge in store."

Greene of course was as eager to be on the march against the bottled-up British as Marion was, and growing more eager each day as Cornwallis' complete defeat became ever more certain. But he was unable to move until help reached him from the North late in October. The newcomers were Colonel Isaac Shelby and Lieutenant Colonel Sevier, with five hundred North Carolina and Tennessee mountain men, some of whom had aided in the dramatic defeat of the British at the Battle of King's Mountain. Presumably Shelby and Sevier also brought with them a goodly supply of shot and powder, enough at least for a certain amount of active fighting by men who knew how to husband their ammunition. At any rate Greene promptly put into action the plan he had had in mind by issuing orders for a new disposition of the Patriot forces.

Greene assigned the new reinforcements to Marion, and early in November the Swamp Fox led his now-formidable body of men south across the Santee. At the same time Sumter moved to Orangeburg to protect that region from Tory raiders, and Pickens moved farther west to put down the Tory-inspired Indian uprisings that had recently been alarming isolated Up Country farmers.

Marion's scouts informed him that Stewart was then encamped with two thousand men at a place called Wantoot, some ten miles north of Monck's Corner and about fifty miles from Charleston. Stewart had already received unofficial news of Cornwallis' defeat and was employing his whole force in a last-minute collection of whatever food and supplies he could seize and send back to Charleston. Marion swung in a wide circle around Wantoot and took up a post at Huger's Bridge fifteen miles to the southeast. There his seven hundred men were closer to Charleston than Stewart was himself, and in an excellent position to raid Stewart's supply trains on their way to the city. Marion was also now close enough to the enemy to tempt them into an engagement for which he was finally equipped.

On November 9, the day Marion set up his new camp, he received official dispatches reporting the surrender of Cornwallis and seven thousand British troops.

That same day a courier brought Marion a document from the Continental Congress, conveying to the partisan general the official thanks of the thirteen colonies "for his wise, decided and gallant conduct, in defending the liberties of his country." The document especially referred to Marion's rescue of Harden's hard-pressed little band, and to his Brigade's honorable role at Eutaw Springs, by commending him "particularly for his prudent and intrepid attack on a body of British troops on the 31st day of August last; and for the distinguished part he took in the battle of 8th Sept."

Marion, who normally entertained guests with a roasted sweet potato served on a rough piece of bark beside the campfire, gave a most uncharacteristic party the following evening.

At a nearby plantation house he played host not only to his own men but to the Patriot ladies and gentlemen of the neighborhood. But, very characteristically indeed, the party did not celebrate his own commendation by Congress. It marked instead the victory over Cornwallis—a victory that Marion readily recognized as a turning point in the war, a sign pointing unmistakably to America's eventual triumph over England.

Nevertheless he was also aware of the vast amount of work still to be done before the enemy would concede final defeat. Early in the morning after his party he was back at his job again, menacing Stewart's line of supply into Charleston and trying to lure Stewart's army out of the protection of its camp so that it might be attacked with some hope of success by the much smaller force Marion himself commanded.

About a week later General Greene left the Santee Hills and started his own ammunitionless army on a march toward Charleston. He still could not attempt to meet the British in open battle. His plan was simply to encamp as near to Charleston as possible and await supplies there, while he counted on Marion to keep Stewart so occupied that he would not move against the weak Continentals. But before Greene could reach the campsite that was his goal, on the Edisto River about thirty miles south of Charleston, Marion lost the services of the whole Shelby-Sevier force and became overnight a weak reed upon whom Greene could no longer depend.

No one seems to know why those five hundred men deserted Marion at a time when their services were so vital to Greene's plan as well as to the safety of Marion and his Brigade. The most likely explanation seems to be that they had grown restive over having taken part in only two small engagements since joining Marion's command. This lack of activity was not Marion's fault. Since the day of his arrival at Huger's Bridge he had been doing his best to tempt Stewart out from behind his defenses. He had feinted at the British, had paraded his small force almost within musket range of their camp. Stewart had consistently refused to accept his challenges. Only long afterward did Marion discover the reason for his enemy's timidity: Stewart's force, known to number two thousand, actually consisted of only half that number of able-bodied soldiers. More than nine hundred of his redcoats were so sick that they were utterly unable to take the field.

But if Marion had been ignorant of Stewart's weakness, the British general now returned the compliment with interest. Unaware that Marion had lost five sevenths of his force, knowing only that he was uncomfortably close—and that Greene was also not far away—Stewart broke camp and retreated toward Charleston. He didn't stop until he reached Goose Creek Bridge about fifteen miles outside the city.

This unmistakable evidence that the British commander heavily overestimated Patriot strength prompted Greene to an audacious move of his own. At the head of a little force of only three hundred men Greene made a dash toward the strong British garrison then stationed at old Dorchester. The officer in command of that post, reflecting Stewart's fears, convinced himself that Greene was about to attack him with an entire army. He destroyed all his supplies, dumped his cannon into the Ashley River and raced his whole garrison the twenty miles to Charleston.

Thus by the first week of December, 1781, practically the entire British force in South Carolina was crowded into that narrow neck of land between the Ashley and the Cooper rivers or encamped on the islands surrounding Charleston harbor. The Patriots could congratulate themselves for having accomplished a great deal of what they had set out to do when they determined to push the enemy eastward out of Carolina into the sea.

But the Patriot leaders were astutely aware that the completion of that task could be as difficult as everything they had achieved up to that point. The timid Stewart had just been replaced by a new commanding general, Alexander Leslie, whose force was formidable in numbers as well as in position. Ships recently arrived in Charleston had increased his British troops to over three thousand, and he commanded at least a thousand uniformed Tories in addition. He had plenty of ammunition for his small arms. He had artillery for his fortifications. Even with a sizable army, and with the assurance of a simultaneous attack by sea, the Patriots would have been doubtful of success in a direct assault upon the city.

The Patriot army was not large. Greene's own forces numbered a scant eight hundred men, each supplied with exactly four rounds of ammunition. Like Marion's partisans, they had no artillery, and like them they now lacked even blankets or cloaks against the increasing winter cold. Greene did hope soon to be reinforced by some Pennsylvania troops released from service farther north since the Battle of Yorktown. But he knew, if the British General Leslie did not, that no French fleet could be counted on to join him in an attack or even to blockade Charleston harbor against the arrival of fresh troops and new supplies. An open assault of the city was therefore out of the question.

Under the circumstances Greene's plans for the future were much what they had been for the past few months: simply to make the British as uncomfortable as possible despite the security of their position.

The enemy's physical discomfort could be achieved by cutting off or severely limiting its sources of supply, and Greene depended largely upon Marion to achieve this purpose. Encamped close to Charleston, in an area from which the British customarily drew considerable stores of rice and cattle, Marion therefore concentrated his efforts on British foraging parties. As usual his small-scale harrying raids were effective—so effective that when Greene received a small supply of powder and lead, in mid-December, he kept none of it for his own troops but sent it all to the partisan commander.

But Greene wished to inflict mental as well as physical discomfort on the British, to intensify the nervousness and anxiety they already felt. He managed to conceal his own lack of strength by keeping Lee's Legion constantly on the move, back and forth in front of Greene's own camp forty-five miles west·

of Charleston, and Marion's camp closer to the city. Probably few British scouts even attempted to slip past Lee's men in an effort to learn the actual number of Patriot troops; none, apparently, succeeded. The British therefore continued to overestimate their enemy and to worry in proportion to their exaggeration.

Greene also planned, this time in cooperation with President Rutledge, another phase of his psychological warfare against the British. It consisted of reorganizing, inside South Carolina, the civil government that had disappeared with the British conquest of the colony. President Rutledge had been granted near-dictatorial powers when he crossed the border into North Carolina just before Charleston fell, and the Patriots had continued to regard him as their chief official throughout his exile. The actual governing of the population, however, had been conducted by the British as long as they were in virtual control of the whole area. But now that the British had been driven into a tiny corner along the seacoast, the rest of the colony had no active governing body at all.

Rutledge knew the necessity of making new laws for the punishment of Tories and the regulation of other war-born situations. He wanted to see the courts re-established for the handling of the countless claims for damages and the return of stolen property. So he agreed with Greene's proposal to reconvene the state legislature. The closer to Charleston it met, Greene pointed out, the more effective an argument it would be for American strength. The location the two men finally chose was the little town of Jacksonborough only thirty miles from the British lines.

Rutledge returned to South Carolina. Greene moved his army across the Edisto and camped six miles below Jacksonborough, right on the road connecting it to Charleston. In spite of the difficulties an election was held. And while not all the eligible voters cast ballots, the various military encampments of South Carolinians did. As might have been expected, most of the senators and representatives voted into office were military men.

Not long after the balloting took place, Francis Marion received a communication requesting his presence at Jacksonborough on January 18, 1782. He had served his state and his cause as General Marion for many months, as Lieutenant Colonel Marion for many months before that. Now once more, as in 1775, he would be serving her as Senator Marion of St. John's parish, Berkeley County.

CHAPTER

XV

Marion's Brigade had contributed enormously toward restoring to South Carolina once more a degree of freedom under which her legislature could reassemble. It was therefore peculiarly ironical that the actual meeting of that legislature resulted in the near-destruction of the Brigade. Marion's command had never been demolished on the battlefield. But his absence from camp in order to take his seat at Jacksonborough brought about the disaster the enemy had never been able to achieve.

The fears of Marion's officers, that his death would mean the end of the Brigade, may not always have been justified. At certain times the unit was perhaps so strong that it would have remained intact at least for a while even without its founder's guiding hand and the force of his personality. The winter of 1781-82 was not one of those times. Since the preceding autumn the Brigade had been so close to dissolution that probably no one but Marion could have held it together at all.

The trouble had begun in September, when large numbers of Tories deserted the British and began to join units like Sumter's and Marion's. In most cases these men had called themselves Tories in the first place only because they believed the Tories would win the war, and they hoped to be numbered among the victors. Now they were calling themselves Patriots for the same reason. When President Rutledge announced that any man who served for six months with the Patriot forces would be regarded, at the war's end, as a Patriot in good standing—regardless of his Tory sympathies earlier in the struggle—these men had rushed to enlist and insure their future safety. They were well fed and warmly dressed. They had suffered few of the privations the partisans had long endured. Understandably enough, they were not very popular among ill-clad, half starved veterans of long months of fighting.

From the very beginning Marion's men had strongly resented these "reformed Tories." Some simply refused to speak to the new arrivals or to associate with them in any way. Others—and they grew more numerous as the autumn wore on—decided that if these new recruits were so eager to show their devotion to the cause, they could do it by assuming the full burden of the fighting. In small angry groups, almost every day, some of Marion's best-seasoned and most stalwart men walked out of camp and started homeward, to enjoy for themselves some of the comforts and peaceful pursuits that most of the "new" Patriots had enjoyed throughout the war.

Marion had watched them go with understanding of their attitude but with very serious concern. Their departure left his Brigade, which was still responsible for guarding the country between Charleston and the Santee, a body of largely untried recruits whose patriotism was at least questionable. Under the circumstances he was uncomfortable about leaving even for a day when the Assembly was called, but he felt he had no choice. His duty as a citizen took precedence in his mind over his duty as a soldier.

For the period of his absence at Jacksonborough he made what seemed to him the wisest possible disposition of the two regiments into which the Brigade had recently been reorganized, one under Colonel Peter Horry's command and the other under Colonel Maham, builder of the tower that brought about the defeat of Fort Watson. Marion stationed the two units at some distance from each other, in order to cover as much territory as possible. And, probably because Maham was also a member of the legislature and would be attending at least some of its sessions, he gave Horry over-all command of both.

But before Marion departed for Jacksonborough, Maham declared that since his own rank was equal to Horry's, he would not submit himself to Horry's orders. Furthermore Maham said he regarded his own regiment as an independent force, rather like Lee's Legion, and not a part of the Brigade at all.

Marion didn't try to press his own authority on the disgruntled officer. He offered instead to present Maham's claims to General Greene at Jacksonborough and leave the matter in his hands. Then, more uneasy than ever, Marion gave express orders that no civilians be allowed to travel up or down the streams along which the two regiments were encamped. Civilian travelers carried rumors, as Marion very well know, and he wanted no rumors of dissension in his Brigade to reach Charleston. They would be too likely to give rise to an attack that his men were in no condition to withstand.

Marion discussed his problem with Greene as soon as he reached Jacksonborough, and Greene seconded Marion's original decision that Horry was entitled to substitute for his absent general as commander-in-chief of both regiments. Marion repeated this to Maham, also then in Jacksonborough, but Maham made it clear that he would not accept Greene's verdict either. Presumably as a gesture of defiance he began to sign passes for river travel to Charleston, and his regimental officers issued them in his absence.

Two weeks after the legislature opened Marion received an urgent letter from Horry. Horry was ill and very troubled. "Colonel Maham interferes with my command so much I can hardly act," he wrote. He reported that "several ladies" had been permitted to go into Charleston on passes signed by Maham, contrary to his own orders, and concluded with a plea that Marion return as quickly as possible. A second letter, reaching Marion the following week, repeated the plea even more desperately.

Marion couldn't leave Jacksonborough. Several important

legislative matters still required his presence. At his request Greene wrote a letter to Maham, urging a more cooperative attitude—a letter that Maham ignored.

Then Marion heard the news that he had been worriedly anticipating ever since he left camp. While he and his fellow legislators were doggedly arguing the Confiscation Act—a bill designed to raise money for carrying on the war by confiscating Tory property—word reached him that a force was on its way out of Charleston with the purpose of destroying his leaderless Brigade. It consisted of two hundred cavalry and five hundred infantry, all well equipped. Their commander was a prominent Massachusetts Tory then in Charleston and eager to try his hand at the destruction of the Swamp Fox—the brilliant Colonel Benjamin Thompson, later to become so famous throughout Europe as both scientist and administrator that he was created Count Rumford of the Holy Roman Empire.

Thompson and his men were a threat of alarming proportions. Greene, always most concerned with military matters, wanted Marion to resume his place immediately at the head of his Brigade. Marion wouldn't desert the Assembly in the midst of its proceedings. He waited until the senators' gravest problems were all settled, and they were almost ready to adjourn, before he set off toward the Santee at top speed. The recalcitrant Maham was with him. They reached the camp of Maham's regiment late in the day of February 24.

Weary as he was, Marion had intended to lead Maham's regiment out within the hour to join Horry's before the enemy could reach that more vulnerable camp, which Horry himself had already left because of his illness. But Maham's staff had just received a report that Thompson had after all changed his mind, and was retreating back toward Charleston.

Marion accepted the report at face value. Gratefully he prepared to enjoy a night's rest, planning to move on and check on the other regiment's safety the following morning. Colonel Maham left to spend the night at his own plantation not far away.

A few hours later a panting courier roused Marion from his exhausted sleep. He had come from Horry's regiment with the staggering news that those green troops had already been overwhelmed by Colonel Thompson's strong force. Forty of Horry's recruits had been killed and thirty-five horses captured before the courier had ridden off, and Thompson had begun to track down the survivors who had fled into the nearby swamps and woods.

Marion spent no futile moments regretting the disintegration of his intelligence network, which under his own direction would almost certainly have prevented the surprise of Horry's men and would have corrected the misinformation received at Maham's camp. Not even waiting for Maham himself to arrive from his plantation, Marion whipped the regiment into action. He was riding at its head when it set off at a furious pace for the scene of the one-sided battle thirty miles away.

He found Thompson still there, still trying to ferret out the fugitives who had escaped his slashing attack. Sending out picked men to skirmish with the surprised redcoats, Marion posted part of his infantry behind a fence and ordered his cavalry to charge the British horse across a clearing in the forest. Even the "new Whigs" in Maham's regiment seemed to acquire confidence from Marion's sure-voiced commands, and spurred their horses straight toward the enemy.

But sudden, wild panic overcame the recently recruited Patriots before they came to grips with Thompson's men. In a churning body they swerved to one side and sought cover in the woods, leaving the clearing open to a British countercharge that drove the American foot soldiers back in a hopeless rout. Marion, inextricably caught up in the panic-stricken dash of his cavalry, was unable to stop their terrified retreat until they were deep in the forest. There he was finally able to restore some degree of order and lead the horsemen out again to check the British pursuit of his foot soldiers.

A Patriot counterattack was out of the question. Marion's only hope was to rescue as many of his men as possible. By skillful use of his reorganized cavalry he did manage to get most of them safely away. But many members of the Brigade jumped into the Santee in the desperate hope of swimming to safety, and of this number some were drowned and others shot from the bank by British marksmen.

Marion's men had often retreated in the past, but always his retreats had been as brilliant as his forays and always he had brought his men off a battlefield with their striking power undiminished and their morale unshaken. This time, as had never occurred in the past, the Brigade had retreated after a real defeat. This time both its striking power and its morale were shattered. One Tory newspaper jubilantly reported, "Colonel Thompson has defeated General Marion in South Carolina, killing one hundred men, and Marion was drowned, attempting to escape." No doubt the exaggeration and the lie were both accepted even by many Patriots. Marion himself, aware that his Brigade was no longer fit to guard the area between Charleston and the Santee, led the remnants of it across the river into the safer haven of Williamsburg.

The destruction of Marion's Brigade had happened at a time when Patriot forces throughout South Carolina seemed to be falling to pieces. Because of continual friction with Greene, Sumter had resigned, and the new commander appointed over his Brigade had so failed to inspire the men's loyalty that Sumter's unit was deteriorating. Because Harden had just resigned, in protest against a new officer named to supersede him, his Brigade had completely disbanded. And because rumors of peace with England had been growing stronger and more numerous, ever since Cornwallis' defeat at Yorktown, the will to restore those forces seemed lacking.

The refusal of many men to fight any longer was certainly understandable, especially after word reached America in April that the British Parliament regarded the fight for the American colonies as a lost cause and had informed the King it would concur in any measure he might take to bring the war to an end. Most people thought General Leslie, the British commander in

Charleston, was accepting the inevitability of defeat when he offered to cease all hostilities, provided only that he be permitted to buy food openly for the troops and Tory civilians still penned up inside the city.

But in the midst of the general rejoicing at the thought of victory and peace, there were some sober Americans who realized that a war ends as slowly as it often begins, and that what appears to be its final months can instead be a period in which the enemy is merely building itself up for another desperate blow. John Mathews, for example, who had been elected the new governor of South Carolina at the expiration of Rutledge's four-year term, feared that Leslie's seemingly innocent request might conceal some such menace, and he refused to allow food for the British to pass through American lines. Leslie promptly countered by threatening to renew active warfare. The number of troops he had in Charleston put sharp teeth into the threat.

The Patriots might have been almost helpless in the face of it. But at that moment Marion let it be known that he was again ready to take the field.

His Brigade had arrived in Williamsburg a mere skeleton, and probably only the potent tonic of Marion's presence could have filled that skeleton out again. But when it had become known that he was again seeking volunteers, men began to reappear by one's and two's at the edge of his campsite. Some were shamefaced, some nonchalant, but all took for granted that Marion would receive them without question. When Marion could count sixty cavalry and forty infantrymen in what had been Maham's regiment, and a hundred or more in Horry's, he had combined the two half-restored units into a single new regiment and recommended to the state president that Maham be its commander.

His preference of Maham over Horry—whom Marion named commandant of Georgetown in amends for the choice—was characteristic of Marion who never let personal feelings interfere with what he believed to be right. Horry had faithfully obeyed him from the moment Marion became his commander.

Maham had flouted his orders publicly and privately. But Maham was a better cavalry officer than Horry, and the Brigade was essentially a cavalry force, and on that basis alone Marion had made what must have been a difficult decision.

As it happened, however, Maham became ill shortly afterward, returned to his plantation and was there surprised by a group of Tories who kept him paroled to his home for the rest of the war. So it was Marion in person who led his newly organized Brigade back across the Santee to protect the region directly north and west of Charleston from British foraging parties. He made camp at Dorchester, from which he could watch the boat traffic on the Ashley River, and sent out detachments to patrol the Cooper and its network of tributary creeks.

Leslie immediately decided that he could do no further foraging in that sector until Marion had left it. To draw Marion away he sent an emissary up to the Pee Dee region to arouse the Tories there once more. Marion's old enemy, the Tory Major Gainey, was one of the first to respond. Ignoring the truce Horry had once made him sign, he assembled a large force and undertook a series of murderous, thieving raids. Marion, of course—just as Leslie had hoped—was ordered to hasten to that region and put a stop to Gainey's activities.

Marion moved his men so fast that no word of his coming preceded him, and near the Pee Dee he divided them into three groups and sent them all simultaneously into Gainey's territory. He hoped by these sudden enveloping tactics to frighten the Tories into submission without the need of firing a shot. He succeeded admirably. The abrupt materialization of three arms of Marion's cavalry startled Gainey completely. Unable to defend himself, the Tory proposed a truce. Marion agreed.

Both officers appointed commissioners to meet and arrange the truce terms, and the meeting duly took place. But the men who sat down to discuss peace had so often faced each other across rifle muzzles that they could not talk rationally together now. The session had to be broken off because they were exchanging blows rather than words.

Gainey's next proposal, that he and Marion themselves confer, was heatedly opposed by Marion's staff. Gainey, they said, was little better than a bandit and Marion would lose face by meeting with him. Marion brushed their objections aside. He had never protected his own dignity at the expense of his men, and he had no intention of standing on dignity now when such a stand could prevent the conclusion of a truce. On June 8, 1782, at a spot not far from where the town of Marion stands today, Gainey signed the terms Marion had dictated. Immediately afterward more than five hundred Tories laid down their arms and promised to live as peaceful citizens of South Carolina, in return for Marion's promise of freedom from retaliation.

Only a few of the most vicious Tories of the area had been barred from taking advantage of the treaty terms, but there were a few others who refused to accept them. And Marion's officers objected again when one of these—a man named Fanning, notorious for his brutality to Patriots—requested a safe-conduct pass to Charleston for his wife and a wagonload of belongings. No concessions whatever, Marion's officers insisted, ought to be made to a man of Fanning's reputation. But once more Marion overrode their protests.

"Let his wife and property reach the British lines," Marion pointed out patiently, "and Fanning will follow. Force them to remain, and we only keep a serpent in our bosom."

He signed the pass. Not long after Mrs. Fanning's departure from the neighborhood, Fanning himself followed, slipping through the American lines to lose himself harmlessly among the British in Charleston.

Marion's determined reassembling of his Brigade had been the act of a man who could not turn aside from a difficult task until that task was finally completed. He had not built up his fighting force again simply to cause further bloodshed. The purpose had been rather to help bring about peace as quickly as possible, and with the least possible spilling of further blood, either Patriot or Tory. But Marion was realizing that certain Patriots were unwilling to stop fighting redcoats, especially Tory redcoats, and that some of those determinedly vengeful men were members of his Brigade. They had argued against signing a truce with Gainey before defeating Gainey first, had argued against giving Fanning the opportunity to escape. And when a Captain Butler, an active Tory raider, appeared in Marion's camp seeking his protection, those same men sent Marion a message saying Butler did not deserve protection—that nothing would save him from the fate his past entitled him to.

Marion read the threat behind the words and correctly interpreted the angry mutterings throughout the camp. His men clearly meant to hang Butler with their own hands if they could seize the opportunity. Quietly Marion reminded the Brigade that Butler had surrendered in reliance on the treaty terms and that the Brigade was bound in honor to protect him. But he also prudently brought Butler into his own tent and posted extra guards around it.

The atmosphere of the whole camp simply grew more tense.

In the past, surrounded by powerful enemies, Marion might have enforced his orders at the point of a bayonet if necessary. Now he was as eager to see the warlike spirit die out among his own Brigade as to see it disappear among the Tories. He called together a few of his most trustworthy friends and had Butler smuggled out of the camp at night to a place from which he could safely leave the region. Then he let his men know that the Tory had gone, and watched with relief and satisfaction as their vindictiveness subsided once its object had been removed from their reach.

In the meantime, back in Charleston, the British General Leslie had not been idle. The moment Marion left the Santee area he had assembled a formidable force of eight hundred men and a fleet of small boats, some equipped with cannon, for a determined foraging expedition.

When Greene heard the news he sent a courier to recall Marion to his Santee River post. Marion had been driving his cavalry hard, and they were in no condition to stand up under another of his forced marches. So he left them behind to rest and police the district, and started off with a new and recently recruited body of men which he reinforced when he reached the Santee.

For a few days he could not learn the object of the first strike by Leslie's fleet. Then came the report that it was heading up the coast to attack Georgetown.

Marion instantly marched his men there at a killing forty-mile-a-day pace but found no sign of the invaders when he arrived. Their absence was explained when a courier informed him that they had instead been sailing up the Santee, where they had collected six hundred barrels of rice from the river plantations before returning to Charleston. Convinced that the foragers' next goal would be the plantations along the Cooper River, Marion back-tracked as swiftly as he had marched coastward, and camped on Wadboo Creek close to its junction with the Cooper's west branch.

Leslie was apparently by then as averse to further bloodshed as Marion himself. At any rate he was trying to keep his foraging parties well away from Patriot-patrolled regions, particularly those patrolled by the Swamp Fox. But Leslie's intelligence network, which had correctly informed him of Marion's wild but useless dash to Georgetown, failed to discover that Marion had dashed back inland again to the Cooper River area. Leslie decided—just as Marion had anticipated he would—to try to obtain the additional rice he needed from the Cooper River plantations. He believed there was a small detachment of Patriots at the Wadboo, but that a quick sortie could disperse them. The party he sent out consisted of a hundred dragoons and some infantry. They were led by the same Major Fraser whose cavalry Marion's Brigade had brilliantly ambushed and cut to pieces a year earlier at Parker's Ferry, thereby rescuing Harden's little band and winning for Marion a citation from Congress.

When one of Marion's outposts rushed into his Wadboo Creek camp with the news that a British force was approaching,

Marion quickly sent out a small group of officers—the only mounted men with him at the time—to scout the enemy. Soon those scouts came thundering back across a big open field with Fraser's full force close behind them. They had been surprised at their task and were being hotly pursued.

Swiftly Marion disposed his forces to meet the new and unexpectedly dangerous situation. He hid a group of infantry behind the low-hanging boughs of a long line of cedars, and a group of riflemen behind several small buildings.

The ambush was quite similar to the one that had defeated Fraser the year before, and again—as on that occasion—Fraser rushed into the trap. The redcoated dragoons churned into a confused mob as men and horses fell. Fraser rallied them and tried another charge. But this time he saw those muzzles protruding menacingly from beneath the cedars, and drew his men off to a safe distance.

Perhaps, then, Fraser remembered Parker's Ferry, recognized the enemy with whom he was dealing, and decided not to risk a complete repetition of that disaster. At any rate he retreated immediately.

Marion's brief second brush with Fraser was, though he could not have been aware of it then, his last military action in the American War for Independence.

Not many days after that short but conclusive affair a huge British fleet dropped anchor in Charleston harbor. It had not come to reinforce the redcoats but to take them away. Charleston was about to change hands once more, this time without fighting. British evacuation of the city, long rumored, was actually to become a fact. Long months dragged by, however, before the occupying force finally left.

As the hot summer of 1782 turned slowly into autumn, Marion remained encamped along Wadboo Creek. British woodgathers and water-barrelers were often in the neighborhood, but Marion prevented his men from troubling them. They would soon be leaving the country, and he wanted only to see them leave in peace. He did more than discourage skirmishes against the little foraging groups. Advised one day that a British watering party near his camp could easily be ambushed, he replied that he had no wish to molest the men—had, in fact, sent out a guard to protect the redcoats at their task.

"My Brigade," Marion told his informer, "is composed of citizens, enough of whose blood has been shed already. If ordered to attack the enemy, I shall obey. But with my consent not another life shall be lost, though the event should procure me the highest honors of the soldier."

Marion, of course, had never cared about collecting honors, and this was as true at the war's end as it had been during his days of active fighting, when he so often retreated—regardless of what other officers might think of his bravery—in order to protect and preserve his Brigade. If he felt any hurt at the order that prohibited all partisans from joining the triumphal Patriot re-entry into Charleston, on December 14, 1782, the hurt was for his men rather than for himself.

Others viewed the exclusion of the partisans on that occasion with more rancor. The state's civil authorities had made the decision, on the grounds that the partisans might cause trouble by fighting with the British who would be embarking from Charleston's wharves while the Americans marched down the neck of the peninsula into the city. Greene vigorously opposed the decree. Moultrie, in his *Memoirs,* refused even to accept the reason given to support it.

Describing the Americans' arrival in Charleston that day, which he viewed as a recently exchanged prisoner of war, he wrote:

> The American regular army entered it in triumph; but our poor partisans were thought *too* irregular, too ragged of raiment to share this triumph! They were not too ragged to *fight,* only too ragged for *show.* It was a most ungenerous and ungrateful exclusion from the scene of the very men to whom the best part of the grand result was due!

It was also Moultrie who best described the end of the partisan Brigades, whose reason for existence had passed with the departure of the enemy from American shores.

"They were disbanded here and there in swamp and thicket," he wrote with unusual simplicity, "wherever the moment found them."

For Marion and his Brigade, the moment found them still on the Wadboo. There, in the shadows of the cedars that had shielded them from Fraser's attack, Marion called the men together. With few exceptions they were not the same ardent Patriots who had first rallied under his leadership at Williamsburg two and a half years earlier. Many of those first men had been killed; others had simply grown too weary to fight that long under such difficult conditions as the Brigade had constantly endured. But even the most recently recruited "new Whigs" among the group had become by now accepted members of this strange, small fraternity. And there could not have been a single man present that day who did not feel the strength of the bond that held Marion's men together—the bond that was Marion himself and the cause he represented to them so clearly by his own devoted service and undeviating faith.

Simply and quietly he thanked them for what they had done. As simply and quietly he told them good-by. Then, with no more pomp and ceremony than had heralded his appearance in the Williamsburg district in the late summer of 1780, he mounted his horse, Ball, and he and Oscar started home to the long-deserted plantation called Pond Bluff.

CHAPTER

XVI

Marion reached home, penniless and over fifty years of age, to find Pond Bluff in ruins. Most plantations in that area along the Santee had been harmed during the war, of course, but none perhaps more than his. A British supply line, so often the focus of bloody raids—some conducted by Marion's own Brigade—had passed within a mile of it. The Battle of Eutaw Springs had been fought within sight of his acres. Tory raiders, throughout the fighting, must have taken particular pleasure in despoiling the property of the dreaded Swamp Fox.

Marion's farm implements were all gone, either converted to Patriot war use, or stolen or destroyed by the enemy. There was no grain left on the farm and no livestock. The buildings he found still standing were in some cases almost in ruins, at best hideously defaced. There was no furniture left, no household utensils of any kind.

But ten of his workmen were still there, having come back from safe hiding places in the swamps. Together they started the long uphill job of restoring the blood-soaked land to productivity.

Marion still could not use all his time and energy for his own interests, however. He continued to serve as a member of the Senate and its sessions were long and difficult. Many problems had to be faced and solved in order to transform a Revolution-torn colony into a peaceful member of the new United States.

And though still uncomfortable as a speech-maker, as always in the past, Marion now sometimes forced himself to speak his mind aloud on a controversial issue.

Having voted in Jacksonborough for the Confiscation Act as a necessary measure for the support of the war, he now took the unpopular stand of defending former Tories whose property had been or was about to be seized. Even his friends could not convince him to change his opinion. He was among them at dinner one night—all of them stanch Confiscation Act supporters except himself—when his host, the governor, called on him for a toast. Marion raised his glass. "Gentlemen," he said with his quiet smile, "here's damnation to the Confiscation Act!"

On another occasion in the Senate itself—and this was a day Marion's friends never forgot—he rose to address the meeting. The subject under discussion was a bill to protect all Patriot officers from claims that might be made against them for food, horses or other supplies which those officers had confiscated during the war. Marion had no objection to the bill itself and said so. Most officers, he believed, had taken civilian property only when it was vital to their forces, and he felt they should not be asked now to pay for their seizures.

"But as for myself," he continued, "if I have given any occasion for complaint, I am ready to answer in property and person. If I have wronged any man I am willing to make him restitution. If, in a single instance, in the course of my command, I have done that which I cannot fully justify, justice requires that I should suffer for it."

The bill was passed. But in the list of officers' names appended to it—officers specifically protected by its measures—Marion's name did not appear. It had been omitted at his own request.

Not long after the war Marion was named commander of Fort Johnson, the little fortification that had originally stood alone as defender of Charleston harbor, and which had recently been regarrisoned. A small salary was attached to the post and little active service was required of him. Presumably his appointment was a gesture on the part of South Carolina to repay him for his long labors on her behalf. It was the only such gesture the state ever made, except for voting him a gold medal—and it is uncertain whether the medal itself was ever presented.

But Marion held the post for only a brief period. Then certain citizens began to complain that Fort Johnson did not need a commandant, that the state could not afford to pay one. Marion quietly resigned. Probably, to avoid embarrassing those who had made the complaints, he gave as his reason the fact that he was about to be married.

Although Francis Marion, unlike his brothers, had always appeared to be a confirmed bachelor, his marriage was no surprise to his friends. Legend says it would never have occurred at all if they had not urged him to it, had not first convinced him that Mary Videau spoke of him often and with great admiration, that she would in fact certainly accept his proposal if he would only make it. She was his cousin, a woman close to his own age. And she did accept him as readily as Marion's friends had assured him she would.

Pond Bluff acquired a new residence after their marriage. It was built of cypress wood left unpretentiously unpainted, but with room enough for the entertainment of the General's friends who were always made welcome there. Mary Videau had, as people said in those days, brought her husband a fine fortune, and the plantation began to flourish again.

But Marion's way of life changed very little. He was still a good planter, still fond of hunting and fishing. He had no desire to spend the summer fashionably in Charleston. He preferred a quiet trip into the hill country, accompanied now by Mary rather than by his troops, but sleeping in the same tent he had used during the war and watching his servant Oscar cook their supper over a familiar fire in the same iron pot.

His neighbors loved him and would have made a hero of him if he had permitted it. Once the people of Georgetown did ignore his well-known preference for retirement by sending a committee to visit him with a tribute they had drawn up to their beloved "Citizen General." Its words were simple because, as they pointed out, "We mean not to flatter you," but they were full of gratitude for the man whose achievements "remain recorded in such indelible characters upon our minds that neither change of circumstances, nor length of time, can efface them."

William Dobein James, who would later write his sketch of Marion and the Brigade, was one of the committee who called on the General that day. Perhaps he wrote the tribute himself. Its final words reflect the same kind of respectful esteem James had always felt for the commander he served as a boy and whom he still remembered admiringly when he himself was an old man.

> Taught by us [the tribute concluded], our children shall hereafter point out the places, and say *"here,* General Marion, posted to advantage, made a glorious stand in defense of the liberties of his country—*there,* on disadvantageous ground, retreated to save the lives of his fellow citizens." What could be more glorious for the General, commanding freemen, than thus to save the lives of his fellow soldiers? Continue, General, in peace, to till those acres which you once wrested from the hands of an enemy. Continue to enjoy dignity accompanied with ease, and to lengthen out your days blessed with the consciousness of conduct unaccused of rapine or oppression, and of actions ever directed by the purest patriotism.

Francis Marion died at Pond Bluff on February 27, 1795. He was buried not far away at Belle Isle Plantation, where he had once lived with his brother.

He left no descendants. No impressive monument preserves the record of his wartime gallantry or his wisdom in time of peace. Even the acres he planted and cared for no longer serve as a memorial to his love of the land and the freedom he sought for it. Those acres now lie beneath the waters of a lake man-made a century and a half after his death, when the Santee River was dammed as part of a government project to provide hydroelectric power for a huge area of South Carolina. The farmers of that area benefit from the new source of power, and Marion would almost certainly approve of that. A better life for planters would undoubtedly seem to him more than a fair exchange for the disappearance of some of the country he knew so well—the country William Cullen Bryant wrote of in his *Song of Marion's Men:*

> Our fortress is the good green wood,
> Our tent the cypress tree;
> We know the forest round us
> As seamen know the sea.
> We know its walls of thorny vines,
> Its glades of reedy grass,
> Its safe and silent islands
> Within the dark morass.

The name of the Swamp Fox still lives in the name of that lake, and South Carolina is no longer the only state that has a town named Marion. So do twenty-four others, all eager to do honor to the Revolutionary hero who cared little for fame even among his own people and who has long since become one of the best-loved heroes of the nation he helped to bring to life.

But perhaps it is in the nameless places where Francis Marion can most easily be recalled today—in sandy country thick with pines and breathless in the heat of noon, on a black waterway threading through a swamp, overhung by tattered ribbons of gray moss and starred with water hyacinths. In the vast stretch of South Carolina now called the Francis Marion National Forest there are many of these empty, quiet places, oases of silence where it is easy to imagine a sudden thunder of hoofs, the clash of sabers and the bark of guns—and then again a silence, quick and complete. It is easy to see

> The glitter of their rifles,
> The scampering of their steeds

—the swift flash of a small, dark man and the ragged Brigade that followed after him on the long, hard road to America's independence.

BIBLIOGRAPHY

Horry, Brigadier-General P. and M. L. Weems. *The Life of General Francis Marion.* Philadelphia, 1809.

James, William Dobein. *A Sketch of the Life of Brig. Gen. Francis Marion and A History of His Brigade, from its Rise in June 1780 until Disbanded in December 1782.* Charleston, 1821; new edition, Marietta, Georgia, 1948.

Moore, Horatio N. *Life and Times of General Francis Marion.* Philadelphia, 1845.

Simms, W. Gilmore. *The Life of Francis Marion.* New York, 1846.

McCrady, Edward. *The History of South Carolina under the Royal Government, 1719-1776.* New York, 1899.

—— *The History of South Carolina in the Revolution, 1775-1780.* New York, 1901.

—— *The History of South Carolina in the Revolution, 1780-1783.* New York, 1902.

Fisher, Sydney George. *The Struggle for American Independence,* 2 vols. Philadelphia, 1908.

Greene, George Washington. *The Life of Nathanael Greene,* 2 vols. New York, 1867-1871.

Lee, Henry. *Memoirs of the War in the Southern Department.* Philadelphia, 1812.

Moultrie, William. *Memoirs of the American Revolution, so far as it related to the States of North and South Carolina and Georgia,* 2 vols. New York, 1802.

Phillips, Ulrich Bonnell. *Life and Labor in the Old South.* Boston, 1949.

Tarleton, Lt. Col. Banastre. *History of the Campaign of 1780-1781 in the Southern Province of America.* London, 1781.

INDEX

Ardesoif, Captain, 68-69

Ball, John Coming, 93-96
Barfield, Captain, 75-76
Beaufort, South Carolina, 24
Bryant, William Cullen, 186
Bull, William, 18-19
Burgoyne, John 56

Camden, South Carolina, 79-80, 107-108, 116, 132-133, 137, 140-141, 149
Campbell, George, 120
Campbell, Lord William, 35-36
Carnes, Patrick, 119-120
Charleston, South Carolina, 12-13, 23-24, 27, 29-39, 42-48, 56-61, 101, 107, 110, 148, 149, 150, 154, 160, 164-165, 174, 176, 177, 179-180
Cherokee Indians, 16-22
Clinton, Sir Henry, 39, 57-64, 68-69, 101, 154
Coates, Lt.-Col., 150-152
Conyers, Daniel, 128
Cordes. *See* Marion, Esther Cordes
Cornwallis, Lord, 63, 67, 70, 77, 79, 83, 91, 101, 105, 115-116, 121, 123, 136-137, 148-149, 154-155, 160, 162
Cowpens, battle of, 122-123

Davie, William Richardson, 77, 79, 101
Dorchester, South Carolina, 28, 57, 155, 164, 175
Doyle, John, 132-133

Estaing, Charles (Count d'Estaing), 51-55
Etchoee (Cherokee village), 21
Eutaw Springs, South Carolina, 157-159, 162, 182

Ferguson, Patrick, 101
Fort Johnson, 27-30, 183-184
Fort Motte, 141-145, 147, 149
Fort Moultrie, 31-39, 40-41, 49, 57, 58
Fort Prince George, 17, 19
Fort Sullivan. *See* Fort Moultrie
Fort Watson, 137-140, 149
Francis Marion National Forest, 186
Fraser, Major C., 155-156, 178-179

Gainey, Major, 73-75, 115, 147, 161, 175-177
Gates, Horatio, 67-71, 77, 79, 82
Georgetown, South Carolina, 15, 24, 26, 68, 111-113, 119-121, 124-125, 137, 147-149, 174, 178, 184
Grant, James, 19-22
Greene, Nathanael, 109-111, 113, 115-116, 121-123, 135, 136-141, 143, 145-146, 147-150, 152, 155, 157-161, 162, 163-166, 170-171, 173, 177

Harrison, Major, 83-84, 128
Harden, William, 149-156, 162, 173
Hampton, Wade, 150
Horry, Hugh, 70, 81, 95, 98, 123
Horry, Peter, 9, 14, 16, 26-27, 34, 66-67, 70, 78-79, 83-84, 112-114, 123, 127, 128, 147, 151, 161, 169-172, 174-175

Huger, Isaac, 18, 57, 60, 66

Jacksonborough, South Carolina, 166-167, 168-170
James, John, 68, 72, 74, 84-88, 90, 92-95, 127, 129
James, William Dobein, 8, 10, 68, 70, 185
Johnson, Baker, 134

Kalb, Johann (Baron Kalb), 66-67
Keowee (Cherokee village), 17
King's Mountain, battle of, 101

Lee, Charles, 31, 38-39, 40-41
Lee, Henry ("Light Horse" Harry), 11, 117-123, 135-140, 141-145, 149, 165
Leslie, Alexander, 110, 164-165, 173-175, 177-178
Lincoln, Benjamin, 42
Lyttleton, William, 18

Maham, Hezekiah, 139-140, 147, 151, 169-172, 174-175
Malmedy, Francis, 158
Mathews, John, 174
Marion, Benjamin (brother), 14
Marion, Esther Cordes (mother), 14-15
Marion, Francis, his place in legend and history, 7-11
  early life, 9, 15-16
  Huguenot ancestry, 12-14
  birth, 14-15
  personality, 7-11, 67-68, 78, 118, 123
  in Indian war, 17-22
  member of S.C. Provincial Congress, 23-26, 30
  captain of S.C. volunteer regiment, 26-30
  member of Revolutionary colonial legislature, 30, 41-42, 50
  promoted to major of Second Regiment, 30
  at defense of Sullivan's Island (Fort Moultrie), 31-39
  approves Declaration of Independence, 41
  transferred to Continental Army, 41
  promoted to lieutenant-colonel, 41-42
  serves under General Lincoln, 42-60
  at battle of Savannah, 51-55
  at defense of Charleston, 56-60
  injured by fall, 59-60
  hides from British, 61
  rejoins Continental Army in North Carolina, 64-69
  assumes leadership of Brigade, 69-71
  defeats Gainey, 73-75
  defeats Barfield, 75-76
  engagement at Nelson's Ferry, 77-82
  scouts Wemyss forces, 83-86
  retreats to north, 86-92
  returns to South Carolina, 92-93
  battle of Shephard's Ferry, 93-96
  defeats Colonel Tynes, 98-99
  establishes Snow Island camp, 100
  success in Williamsburg district, 101
  pursued by Tarleton, 102-105
  named "Swamp Fox," 105
  harries enemy supply lines, 106-109
  correspondence with Greene, 110
  fails in Georgetown attack, 111-113
  joined by "Light Horse" Harry Lee, 116-117
  fails in second Georgetown attack, 119-121
  raiding tactics, 123-127
  campaign against Watson, 128,132
  loss of Snow Island camp, 132-133
  rejoined by Lee, 135
  besieges Fort Watson, 137-140

[189]

Marion, Francis (*continued*)
  besieges Fort Motte, 141-145
  controversy with Greene, 145-146
  takes Georgetown, 147-148
  fights under Sumter, 149-150
  rescues Harden's Brigade, 155-156
  battle of Eutaw Springs, 157-159
  guards north bank of Santee, 161
  harries Stewart, 162-164
  honored by Continental Congress, 162
  celebrates victory at Yorktown, 163
  harries British foraging parties, 165-166
  elected to reassembled S.C. legislature, 167
  dissention among his officers, 168-171
  his Brigade defeated by Thompson, 171-173
  subdues Tories in Williamsburg district, 174-177
  harries Leslie's foraging parties, 178-179
  final engagement in Revolution, 178-179
  last days of Brigade, 180
  Brigade barred from triumphal entry into Charleston, 180
  disbands Brigade, 181
  returns to Pond Bluff plantation, 182
  serves in post-war legislature, 182-184
  commands Fort Johnson, 183-184
  marries Mary Videau, 184
  honored by Georgetown friends, 184-185
  death, 185
  posthumous honors, 186
Marion, Gabriel (grandfather), 12-15
Marion, Gabriel (father), 14-16
Marion, Gabriel (brother), 14-15
Marion, Gabriel (nephew), 34, 112-113
Marion, Isaac (brother), 14, 25
Marion, Job (brother), 14, 24, 25
Marion, Louisa (grandmother), 12, 14
Marion, Mary (wife), 184
Marion, South Carolina, 176, 186
McCottry, William, 129-130
McDonald, Sergeant, 115, 131
McKay, James, 138-139
McLeroth, Major, 125-127
McPherson, Lieutenant, 142-144
Melton, John, 112
Monck's Corner, 58, 124, 147-148, 150, 155, 159, 160
Morgan, Dan ("Old Wagoner"), 116, 121-122
Motte, Mrs. Rebecca, 142, 144
Moultrie, William, 8, 18, 24, 30-39, 41, 42-49, 51, 55, 57, 180-181
Mouzon, Henry, 93

Nelson's Ferry, South Carolina, 79-82, 116, 121, 125, 147, 160
Ninety-Six, South Carolina, 115-116, 121, 137, 147-149

Oscar (Marion's servant), 61, 65-66, 147, 181, 184

Parker, Sir Peter, 35-36, 42
Parker's Ferry, South Carolina, 156, 178-179
Pickens, Andrew, 18, 149, 157
Pond Bluff (Marion's plantation), 15-16, 61, 181, 182, 184-185
Postell, James, 123-124
Postell, John, 111-114, 123-125
Prevost, Augustine, 43-49, 51-56
Pulaski, Casimir, 42-43, 45, 47, 54-55

Rawdon, Lord Francis, 137, 140-141, 143, 147-148, 149-150, 152, 157
Rudulph, Michael, 119-120

Rutledge, John, 30, 32, 37-39, 46, 59-60, 65, 66, 68-69, 71, 78, 161, 166, 168, 174

Santee, the High Hills of, 140-141, 163
Savannah, battle of, 51-56
Sevier, Lt.-Col., 161-163
Shelby, Isaac, 161-163
Snow Island (Marion's headquarters), 97-98, 100, 108, 110-111, 121, 132-133
Song of Marion's Men, 186
Stewart, Alexander, 149-150, 157-160, 162-164
Sumter, Thomas, 60, 77, 79, 101, 105, 106, 113, 127-128, 141, 148, 149-150, 161, 162, 173

Tarleton, Banastre, 10-11, 58, 60, 62, 66, 79, 102-106, 122, 127
Thompson, Benjamin, 171-173
Tynes, Colonel, 98-99

Videau, Mary. *See* Marion, Mary

Washington, George, 14, 27-28, 31, 40, 42, 50, 56, 67, 154-155, 160
Washington, William, 121
Watson, John, 121, 128-132, 137, 141
Weems, Mason L., 9-10, 14
Wemyss, James, 83-87, 90, 92-93, 96
Williams, Otho, 67-68
Williamsburg district, South Carolina, 68-72, 147-148, 174, 181
Winnsboro, South Carolina, 101, 105, 116
Witherspoon, Gavin, 134

About the Authors

BERYL WILLIAMS and SAMUEL EPSTEIN are a husband and wife writing team. Together they have written more than fifty books, half of them fiction, the rest non-fiction in various fields, especially biography. Beryl Williams was born in Columbus, Ohio, attending schools there and in Passaic, New Jersey. After graduation from Douglass College, she became a reporter for the New Brunswick *Daily Home News* and the *Sunday Times*. Since 1941 she has been a free-lance writer and editor and has written stories and articles for national magazines. Samuel Epstein was born in Boston, Massachusetts, went to various schools in New York City, New Jersey, Florida, and graduated from Rutgers University. Before devoting himself entirely to books, he did publicity work for an engineering firm, taught at the New York State Training School for Boys, was science editor at the New Jersey Agricultural Experiment Station and a technical writer for the Signal Corps of the U. S. Army.